Public Financial Management

The **General Secretariat of the Public Financial Management Reform Steering Committee (GSC)** is an executive body of the Public Financial Management Reform Steering Committee (PFMR-SC) of the Government of the Kingdom of Cambodia (GoKC), chaired by the Deputy Prime Minister and Minister of Economy and Finance. The main responsibility of GSC is to lead, manage and coordinate the formulation and implementation of this public financial management (PFM) reform program. Specifically, GSC monitors and evaluates the progress and provides policy recommendations to the PFMR-SC, and coordinates the reform implementation with the working groups under the Ministry of Economy and Finance, Line Ministries, and Capital/Provincial Administrations. It also coordinates with development partners to mobilize resources, both financial and technical, to support the program.

The Public Financial Management Reform Program, which was introduced in late 2004, is a core reform program of the GoKC. Its prime objective is to solve the country's chronic budget shortage and other PFM-related issues in Cambodia. Building a sound PFM system is considered the backbone of implementing the GoKC's policy agenda to become an "Upper-middle income" country by 2030 and a "High-income" country by 2050. It also supports other reform programmes to promote inclusiveness, efficiency, effectiveness and accountability in service delivery to people.

The **ISEAS – Yusof Ishak Institute** (formerly Institute of Southeast Asian Studies) is an autonomous organization established in 1968. It is a regional centre dedicated to the study of socio-political, security, and economic trends and developments in Southeast Asia and its wider geostrategic and economic environment. The Institute's research programmes are grouped under Regional Economic Studies (RES), Regional Strategic and Political Studies (RSPS), and Regional Social and Cultural Studies (RSCS). The Institute is also home to the ASEAN Studies Centre (ASC), the Singapore APEC Study Centre and the Temasek History Research Centre (THRC).

ISEAS Publishing, an established academic press, has issued more than 2,000 books and journals. It is the largest scholarly publisher of research about Southeast Asia from within the region. ISEAS Publishing works with many other academic and trade publishers and distributors to disseminate important research and analyses from and about Southeast Asia to the rest of the world.

Public Financial Management
Cambodian Experiences

by
The General Secretariat of Public Financial
Management Reform Steering Committee

edited by
Vinel YETH, Youthy UM and Penghuy NGOV

First published in Singapore in 2023 by
ISEAS Publishing
30 Heng Mui Keng Terrace
Singapore 119614
E-mail: publish@iseas.edu.sg
Website: http://bookshop.iseas.edu.sg

and

Ministry of Economy and Finance, Cambodia
Street 92, Sangkat Wat Phnom
Khan Daun Penh
Phnom Penh
Cambodia
E-mail: admin@meh.gov.kh
Website: https://mef.gov.kh/

All rights reserved. No part of this publication may be reproduced, stored in a retrieval system, or transmitted in any form or by any means, electronic, mechanical, photocopying, recording or otherwise, without the prior permission of the ISEAS – Yusof Ishak Institute and the Ministry of Economy and Finance, Cambodia.

© 2023 ISEAS – Yusof Ishak Institute, Singapore, and Ministry of Economy and Finance, Cambodia

The responsibility for facts and opinions in this publication rests exclusively with the authors and their interpretations do not necessarily reflect the views or the policy of the publishers or their supporters.

ISEAS Library Cataloguing-in-Publication Data

Name(s): Cambodia. General Secretariat of Public Financial Management Reform Steering Committee, author. | Yeth, Vinel, editor. | Um, Youthy, editor. | Ngov, Penghuy, editor.
Title: Public financial management : Cambodian experiences / by General Secretariat of Public Finance, edited by Vinel Yeth, Youthy Um and Penghuy Ngov.
Description: Singapore : ISEAS – Yusof Ishak Institute ; Cambodia : Ministry of Economy and Finance, 2023. | Includes bibliographical references and index.
Identifiers: ISBN 9789815104073 (soft cover) | ISBN 9789815104080 (ebook PDF)
Subjects: LCSH: Finance, Public—Cambodia. | Cambodia—Economic policy. | Cambodia—Politics and government.
Classification: LCC HJ1360.3 C15P97

Cover design by Mardy Chhun
Index compiled by Raffaie Nahar
Typeset by Superskill Graphics Pte Ltd
Printed in Singapore by Mainland Press Pte Ltd

Contents

List of Figures viii

List of Tables x

Foreword xi

Preface xiv

Acknowledgements xvi

Notes on the Author, Editors and Contributors xvii

Abbreviations xix

Chapter 1: Introduction 1
1.1 Background 1
1.2 What Is PFM? 1
1.3 Global Trend of PFM Reform 3
1.4 Scope and Structure 6
Notes 7

Chapter 2: Overview of Cambodian Economy and PFM
 Reform Program 8
2.1 Historical Overview of the Cambodian Economy 8
2.2 Public Finance in Cambodia 11
2.3 PFM Reform Program in Cambodia 13
2.4 PFM and Development Partners' Cooperation 17
2.5 Reform Approach 21
2.6 Achievements, Challenges and Ways Forward 23
2.7 PFMRP Impact on the Cambodian Budget System 30

2.8	Cross-Cutting Reform Programs	36
2.9	Summary	40
Notes		41

Chapter 3: Strategic Planning and Budgeting — 42

3.1	Medium-Term Fiscal Framework	43
3.2	Medium-Term Budget Framework	43
3.3	Budget Strategic Plan	46
3.4	Annual Budgeting	47
3.5	Summary	54
Notes		56

Chapter 4: Components of PFM in Cambodia — 57

4.1	Revenue Management	57
4.2	Public Expenditure Management	67
4.3	Public Investment Management	70
4.4	Public Debt Management	74
4.5	State Property Management	75
4.6	Public Procurement Management	75
4.7	Public Accounting System	77
4.8	Financial Management Information System (FMIS)	81
4.9	Control Systems	93
4.10	Summary	96
Notes		97

Chapter 5: PFM System Assessment Tools — 99

5.1	Public Expenditure and Financial Accountability Framework	99
5.2	Open Budget Survey	112
5.3	Public Investment Management Assessment	116
5.4	Tax Administration Diagnostic Assessment Tool	120
5.5	Summary	121
Notes		123

Chapter 6: Case Study — 124

| 6.1 | PFMRP and Impact on MOEYS | 124 |
| 6.2 | PFMRP and Impact on Ministry of Rural Development | 128 |

6.3	PFM System at Subnational Administration	132
6.4	Summary	135
Note		136

Chapter 7:	PFM Experiences of Selected ASEAN and OECD Countries	137
7.1	Thailand: Strategic Performance-Based Budgeting	137
7.2	Vietnam: Public Investment Management	140
7.3	The Philippines: Decentralization	143
7.4	Malaysia: Outcome-Based Budgeting	146
7.5	Indonesia: New Financial System Called SPAN	149
7.6	New Zealand: Outcome-Focus Management	152
7.7	France: Performance Budgeting	156
7.8	Australia: Performance Budgeting	160
7.9	Sweden: Gender Budgeting	163
7.10	Estonia: e-Government	165
7.11	Lessons Learnt	167
Notes		169

Bibliography   173

Glossary   177

Index   183

List of Figures

2.1	Roles and Responsibilities of GSC	17
2.2	Five Strategies under PFMRP	28
2.3	Budget System Reform	42
3.1	Budget Preparation Cycle	48
3.2	Budget Structure	49
3.3	Annual Budget Cycle	50
3.4	Linkage of National Priorities and Sector Policies	51
3.5	Linkage-Organizational Structure, Role and Responsibility and Program Structure	51
3.6	Program Budgeting Structure	54
3.7	Example: Program Budget for Ministry of Education, Youth and Sports	55
4.1	Current Revenue Achievements, 2013–18	58
4.2	Custom and Excise Revenue, 2013–18	62
4.3	Tax Revenue, 2013–18	64
4.4	Comparison of Transportation Improvements	69
4.5	Spending as a Percentage of GDP and National Budget	71
4.6	Timeline for the Development of Accrual-Based Accounting	80
4.7	FMIS System Outline	82
4.8	Modelling for FMIS and Interfacing	84
4.9	Overview of Budget Allocation Module	85
4.10	Overview of Workflow for Accounts Receivable	85
4.11	Overview of Workflow for Accounts Payable	86
4.12	Overview of Cash Management	87
4.13	Overview of Purchase Order	88

4.14	Overview of General Ledger	89
4.15	Seven Budget Classifications	91
5.1	Interrelationship with the Seven Pillars of PEFA	101
5.2	Trend in Scoring of Public Availability of Budget Information	115
5.3	PIMA Framework	118
5.4	Institutional Strength and Effectiveness of PIM Institutions in Cambodia	119

List of Tables

2.1	Economic Development, 1993–2019	10
2.2	Fiscal Performance, 1993–2002 (KHR billion)	13
2.3	Public Finance	13
5.1	PEFA Pillars and Indicators	104
5.2	Change in Performance Between 2010 and 2015	108

Foreword

Cambodia has come a long way in its nation-building process following its tragic history under the horrendous collectivized management of the Khmer Rouge in the late 1970s. The rehabilitation process had to start from scratch in the 1980s. Cambodia needed to prevent the return of the Khmer Rouge regime while at the same time building the necessary physical infrastructure and human capital. After the official end of the civil war in the late 1990s, the Royal Government of Cambodia (RGC) announced full and complete peace in the whole country. Under the prudent leadership of Samdech Akka Moha Sena Padey Techo Hun Sen, Prime Minister of the Kingdom of Cambodia, and with peace as a necessary precondition, Cambodia has achieved remarkable economic growth in the past decades. Cambodia has also actively engaged in regional and international trade and has become one of the most open economies in the region.

The general election in 1993 marked a new chapter for Cambodia. In the first legislature of the National Assembly, the government adopted a comprehensive macroeconomic policy and structural reform program, which included efforts to integrate the Cambodian economy into the region and the world. Subsequently, the government achieved impressive results, especially in liberalization reforms and economic stabilization, which led to rapid economic growth with a low annual inflation rate below 5 per cent that still stands today.

As the focus was placed on macroeconomic growth and stability, measures to strengthen public financial management (PFM) remained weak. Good governance in PFM remained a major concern, both from the perspectives of revenue mobilization and expenditure efficiency. This situation underlined the need to push for more in-depth and comprehensive reform.

In 2004, the RGC launched a long-term and comprehensive PFM reform program covering both the national and subnational levels. Based on the Cambodian context and drawing on international experiences. This initiative aimed to gradually change government budgeting from an input-based and centralized budget system towards a more performance-based and decentralized budget management system. This program had four phases, the first of which, from 2005 to 2008, focused on strengthening budget credibility. The second phase ran from 2009 to 2015 and aimed at strengthening financial accountability. The third phase (2016–20), which is currently under implementation, focuses on budget-policy linkages. Finally, the fourth phase, to be implemented upon completion of the third phase, will seek to build performance accountability into the budget process. To create a robust foundation for the fourth phase, the PFM Reform Steering Committee has decided to extend the third phase for two more years until 2022 so that the fourth phase is expected for implementation by 2023–27.

Remarkable results have been achieved from the PFM reform effort in the last fifteen years and PFM reform is becoming the backbone of other critical public sector reforms of the government. The government has built the foundation of budget credibility by strengthening state budget revenue collection mechanisms, managing expenditure efficiency, taming public debt, and eliminating chronic payment arrears. The continuous increase in revenue, especially from 2013 to 2021, has enabled the government to significantly increase expenditures for improving the quality and expanding the scope of public services.

At the same time, the government has built the core mechanism of financial accountability by launching Financial Management Information System (FMIS) in all line ministries, expanding FMIS scope across the country, strengthening internal audit functions in line ministries, preparing, improving and strengthening the enforcement of related laws and regulations.

Regarding the linkage between budget and policy, the government has finished implementing a full-fledged program of budgeting in all line ministries and the capital-provincial administrations. In this regard, budget preparation and negotiation have been further strengthened and improved by better reflecting the key priorities of the government's policy. Dissemination of budget information has also been further enhanced by the provision of budget figures in all budget cycles, from the formulation of the macroeconomic framework to the adoption and implementation of the annual budget law. This contributes to the improved efficiency, accountability, and transparency of the budget.

The global COVID-19 pandemic has severely impacted public health and the economy worldwide since early 2020, and Cambodia is not an exception. To mitigate its impact, the RGC took a decisive step by temporarily closing international borders and domestic travel restrictions in high-risk areas. Simultaneously, the government continues to stand firm with confidence and take timely actions to manage public health and the national economy with its aggressive vaccination campaign which later proved effective. The outcome of this effective response to the crisis is also dependent on the robustness of the PFM system. This situation has manifested itself in the results derived from past reforms. It also renews the government's commitment to PFM reform to accelerate higher economic growth and provide better public service delivery to the people.

Despite what we have achieved, much remains to be done. It is also clear that there are still many challenges facing PFM systems that will require concerted efforts by all relevant agencies to make the PFM system a strong, transparent and accountable one so that it can effectively respond to the priorities and the needs of the country's development goals.

Dr AUN Pornmoniroth
Deputy Prime Minister
Minister of Economy and Finance and
Chairman of PFM Reform Steering Committee
Phnom Penh, 3 October 2022

Preface

Cambodia has achieved remarkable economic development, with an average annual GDP growth rate of 7 per cent in the past two decades. A series of reforms have been implemented to support this sustained and robust growth. Among them, public financial management (PFM) reform has played a crucial role and acted as the backbone of all reform efforts. Before the start of PFM reform in the mid-2000s, cash shortages were chronic and arrears in salary payments to civil servants and armed forces were rampant in the country. Inefficiency in budget allocation, which negatively affected the quality of public service delivery, was at a critical level.

Recognizing the need to strengthen the PFM system to improve accountability, efficiency and effectiveness, the government initiated a comprehensive reform program covering all PFM components in 2004. These included macroeconomic policy and the revenue-expenditure framework, public investment management, public debt management, state asset management, public procurement management, the public accounting system, the financial management information system and the fiduciary control system.

Since its inception, the PFM reform program has yielded many positive results. The significant increase in tax revenue, coupled with a transparent and effective revenue management system, enabled the government to allocate more resources to priority sectors, such as health and education, and increase support for other critical public sector reforms. It also spurred a significant increase in civil servants' salaries, which are now paid in a timely manner through banking systems.

In this context, the new spirit of PFM reform is indispensable. The PFM system cannot be robust on its own or without all parties' participation, especially the civil servants who implement it directly. However, general understanding and knowledge of PFM are limited, both among government officials and the general public, posing a challenge on the path to a robust, responsive, transparent and accountable PFM system. This situation has prompted the General Secretariat of the PFM Reform Steering Committee to make greater efforts to raise awareness and promote understanding of PFM.

The *Public Financial Management: Cambodian Experiences* book is one of the new initiatives to address the challenges mentioned earlier. The book starts with an overview of PFM in Cambodia, with a brief introduction to the discipline of public financial management. It goes on to discuss Cambodia's experience implementing PFM reform in detail, including how PFM has reformed government budgeting and how reform impacts the many components of PFM. Finally, case studies of Cambodian reform efforts and selected ASEAN countries (namely, Thailand, Vietnam, the Philippines, Malaysia and Indonesia) and selected OECD countries (namely, New Zealand, Australia, France, Sweden and Estonia) experiences with PFM reform are presented.

This handbook was prepared by the General Secretariat of the PFM Reform Steering Committee with inputs from the European Union, the World Bank, and the International Monetary Fund. We hope that this book will become a simple and effective knowledge-sharing tool for civil servants and the public.

ROS Seilava
Secretary-General,
General Secretariat of PFM Reform Steering Committee,
Ministry of Economy and Finance
Phnom Penh, 5 October 2022

Acknowledgements

The authors would like to express our deepest appreciation to the management of the General Secretariat of PFM Reform Steering Committee (GSC) for supporting the writing of this book. Our special thanks also go to the European Union Commission for their financial and technical assistance.

We also would like to thank Mr Mardy Chhun, who has tirelessly consolidated the draft manuscript from all the contributors to this writing. Our thanks to Mr Terry O'Donnell for technical support in the early stage of the writing process.

The authors also benefit greatly from the constructive comments from our development partners including Mr Javier Castillo (European Union), Mr Chamroeun Ouch (Asian Development Bank), Mr Kimsong Chea (UNICEF), and Mr Suhas Joshi (International Monetary Fund). We are also thankful for the proofreading provided by the World Bank team, especially Dr Sokbunthoeun So, Dr Lindley Higgins, Mr So Seyama and Mr Menghun Kaing.

This book is edited by Mr Vinel Yeth, Mr Youthy Um and Dr Penghuy Ngov.

Notes on the Author, Editors and Contributors

The Author
The *General Secretariat of Public Financial Management Reform Steering Committee* is coordinating the work with the Public Financial Management Reform Working Group of the line ministries and all entities under the Ministry of Economy and Finance and coordinating the cooperation between the Royal Government and development partners under public financial management reform program and coordinating the work with the other reforms of the Royal Government.

The Editors
Mr Yeth Vinel obtained his MBA from RMIT University (Australia) in 2007. He has more than ten years of experience as a budget practitioner within the Ministry of Economy and Finance, Cambodia. Mr Yeth is currently an Under-Secretary of State of the Ministry of Economy and Finance and also a Deputy Secretary General of the General Secretariat of Public Financial Management Reform Steering Committee (GSC), overseeing the overall implementation of the PFM reforms program in the country. With his first-hand and deep knowledge both at the strategic and implementation levels, this book was able to provide detailed information where almost impossible for outsiders.

Mr Um Youthy graduated with an MA Degree from Nagoya University (Japan) in 2013. Mr Um is currently the Head of Administration, Finance, Monitoring, and Evaluation Division of the PFM Reform Steering Committee. He is in charge of monitoring and evaluation of implementing consolidated action plan under the PFM reform program, providing day-to-day operational support to PFM implementers, and coordinating with development partners in terms of financial and technical support to the reform program. His indispensable knowledge and experience in the field have greatly contributed to the writing of this book.

Dr Ngov Penghuy received his PhD from Nagoya University (Japan) in the field of development economics in 2011. After teaching at Nagoya University for six years (2008–2014), he returned to Cambodia and served as the Director and Designated Associate Professor of Nagoya University's Satellite Campus. Since then, he has been actively involved in policy discussions with the Cambodian government. Dr Ngov has extensive knowledge of the Cambodian economy, including the public sector economy. He is also currently a freelance consultant for the General Secretariat of the PFM Reform Program (GSC), where he provides support and advice on a wide range of economic issues.

The Contributors
Sovannara Huy, Senior PFM Specialist
Sophorn Ouch, Senior PFM Specialist
Malimchheng Yorn, Senior PFM Specialist
Mardy Chhun, Senior PFM Specialist
Sungchheang Kang, Senior PFM Specialist
Vong Ly, Senior PFM Specialist
Chakriya Sokun, Senior PFM Specialist
Laiheng Pom, Senior PFM Specialist
Soyaro Heang, Senior PFM Specialist
Makara Ung, Senior PFM Specialist
Ramorn Meth, Senior PFM Specialist
Chhomkeovoleak Kong, Senior PFM Specialist
Sokmai Pheng, Senior PFM Specialist
Dalin Ros, Senior PFM Specialist
Sokheng Lem, Senior PFM Specialist
Sokpheng Chea, Senior PFM Specialist
Sattra Vuthy, PFM Specialist
Kimheng Sun, PFM Specialist
Sovandy Loeung, PFM Specialist
Ratha Sron, PFM Specialist
Voleaktevy Ung, Assistant to PFM Specialist
Changphuong Leng, Assistant to PFM Specialist
Virasak Sokun, Assistant to PFM Specialist

Abbreviations

ABB	Accrual-Based Budgeting
ACCA	Association of Chartered Certified Accountants
ADB	Asian Development Bank
AM	Aide Memoire
BAPPENAS	Ministry of National Development Planning or National Development Planning Agency [Indonesia]
BESF	Budget of Expenditures and Sources of Financing
BPR	Business Process Reengineering
BSP	Budget Strategic Plan
CAP	Consolidated Action Plan
CDC	Council for the Development of Cambodia
COA	Chart of Accounts
COM	Council of Ministers
COVID-19	Novel Coronavirus
CPD	Continuous Professional Development
CPSAS	Cash Basis Cambodian Public Sector Accounting Standards
D&D	Decentralization and De-concentration
DAC	Development Assistance Committee
DI	Department for Investment
DP	Development Partner (includes Donor Agencies)
EA	Executing Agency
EB	Enacted Budget
EBA	Everything But Arms
EBP	Executive's Budget Proposal
EFI	Economics and Finance Institute
EO	Executive Order

EU	European Union
FAD	Financial Affairs Department
FDI	Foreign Direct Investment
FMIS	Financial Management Information System
FMM	Financial Management Manual
FMWG	Financial Management Working Group
FTA	Free Trade Agreement
FTE	Fiscal Transparency Evaluation
GAB	General Appropriations Bill
GAP	Gender Action Plan
GB	Gender Budgeting
GDB	General Department of Budget
GDCE	General Department Customs and Excise
GDICDM	General Department of International Cooperation and Debt Management
GDNT	General Department of National Treasury
GDP	Gross Domestic Product
GDPP	General Department of Public Procurement
GDSNAF	General Department of Subnational Administration Finance
GDT	General Department of Taxation
GIFMIS	Government Integrated Financial Management Information System
GIFT	Global Initiative for Fiscal Transparency
GSC	General Secretariat of Public Financial Management Reform Steering Committee
GSP	Generalized Scheme of Preferences
KHR	Khmer Riel
IA	Implementation Agency
IAS	International Accounting Standards
IBP	International Budget Partnership
IFI	Independent Fiscal Institution
IFMIS	Integrated Financial Management Information System
IFRS	International Financial Reporting Standards
IMF	International Monetary Fund
INTOSAI	International Organization of Supreme Audit Institutions

IPSAS	International Public Sector Accounting Standards	
IT	Information Technology	
IYRs	In-Year Reports	
JCPPR	Joint Country Portfolio Performance Review	
JICA	Japan International Cooperation Agency	
LGU	Local Government Unit	
LM	Line Ministry	
LMIC	Lower Middle-Income Country	
LOLF	*Loi Organique des Lois de Finances* (Organic Law of Finance)	
MBS	Modified Budget System	
MDB	Multi-lateral Development Banks	
MDG	Millennium Development Goals	
MEF	Ministry of Economic and Finance	
MFO	Major Final Outputs	
MIP	Multiannual Indicative Programme	
MLOVT	Ministry of Labour and Vocational Training	
MOEYS	Ministry of Education, Youth, and Sport	
MOP	Ministry of Planning	
MOU	Memorandum of Understanding	
MTBF	Medium-Term Budget Framework	
MTEF	Medium-Term Expenditure Framework	
MTFF	Medium-Term Fiscal Framework	
MYR	Mid-Year Review	
NAA	National Audit Authority	
NBC	National Bank of Cambodia	
NEDA	National Economic Development Authority	
NGAS	New Government Accounting System	
NPE	New Political Economy	
NPFM	New Public Financial Management	
NRMIS	Non-Tax Revenue Management Information Technology	
NSDP	National Strategic Development Plan	
NTP	National Transformation Program	
O&M	Operation and Maintenance	
OBB	Outcome-Based Budgeting	
OBI	Open Budget Index	

OBS	Open Budget Survey
ODA	Official Development Assistance
OECD	Organization for Economic Cooperation and Development
OGP	Open Government Partnership
OPIF	Organization Performance Indicator Framework
OSP	Official Crude Pricing
PAE	Public Administration Entities
PAR	Public Administration Reform
PARMP	Public Administration Reform Master Plan
PAS	Public Administration System
PAT	Partnership for Accountability and Transparency
PB	Program Budgeting
PBB	Performance-Based Budgeting
PBS	Pre-Budget Statement
PD	Project Director
PEFA	Public Expenditure and Financial Accountability
PFM	Public Financial Management
PFMRC	Public Financial Management Reform Commission
PFMRP	Public Financial Management Reform Program
PFMR-SC	Public Financial Management Reform Steering Committee
PIB	Performance-Informed Budgeting
PIM	Public Investment Management
PIMA	Public Investment Management Assessment
PIP	Public Investment Program
PIU	Project Implementation Unit
PM	Procurement Manual
PM	Project Manager
PRC	Procurement Review Committee
PRK	People's Republic of Kampuchea
PT	Provincial Treasury
PV	Public Value
RA	Reform Act
RGC	Royal Government of Cambodia
ROI	Return on Investment

RS	Rectangular Strategy
SAI	Supreme Audit Institution
SARMIS	State Asset Register Management Information System
SDR	Special Drawing Rights
SIDA	Swedish International Development Cooperation Agency
SNA	Subnational Administration
SNG	Subnational Government
SOE	State-Owned Enterprise
SOP	Standard Operating Procedures
SPBB	Strategic Performance-Based Budgeting
SPFMP	Strengthening Public Financial Management Program
SPPIM	Standard Procedures for Public Investment Management
SRA	Strategic Result Areas
TADAT	Tax Administration Diagnostic Assessment Tool
TA	Technical Assistance
TOR	Terms of Reference
TTT	Training and Technology Transfer
UN	United Nations
UNICEF	United Nations Children's Fund
UNTAC	United Nations Transitional Authority in Cambodia
WB	World Bank
WHO	World Health Organization
WTO	World Trade Organization
YER	Year-End Report

CHAPTER ONE

Introduction

1.1 BACKGROUND

The Royal Government of Cambodia (RGC) has achieved substantial progress in public financial management (PFM) since the inception of the reform program in 2004. PFM is the backbone of RGC reforms, but its objectives and benefits are not widely known to the public. While many components of PFM are present throughout the government, the overall system and its benefits are not widely understood or recognized. This is, in part, due to the holistic and long-term successes of PFM reform in Cambodia having never been described in one place.

This book offers a remedy to this problem by providing an overview of PFM and Cambodia's reform experiences. This examination includes a recent history of PFM reform, a delineation of its components in the RGC, a discussion of how PFM affects planning and budgeting, case studies within the RGC, and a comparison of reform experiences of selected OECD and ASEAN countries. Finally, the book draws key lessons from reform experiences (successes and failures) in both developed and developing countries that may be useful in the Cambodian context.

1.2 WHAT IS PFM?

PFM can be explained with a simple analogy as the following. In everyday life, each household is faced with questions about earned income and spending. These questions may include:

- What do we need with regard to food, clothes, education and entertainment?

- Where does the money come from to pay for it?
- Do we have enough money to cover all the expenses we need? Should we borrow money from somewhere? Are we able to pay back our borrowed loan?
- Is everyone in the family adequately taken care of?

These questions are familiar to every household and if we do not properly address them can lead to dire consequences for the family.

A government is like a household, but larger. Every citizen is a family member of that household. The process by which the government manages its resources to meet the needs of its citizens is called Public Financial Management (PFM). In a family, parents work and get paid, and this may constitute the whole income for the household. The government gets its revenue from tax and non-tax sources domestically and from external sources, such as loans and grants from bilateral[1] and multilateral[2] aid agencies. The government wants to use its revenues efficiently, equitably and in a manner that provides stability and sustainability of the operation of the government.

Sound management of government revenue and expenditure is the key to maintaining good fiscal discipline. It contributes to establishing a stable environment for growing businesses, maintaining good living standards, promoting sustainable economic development and providing protection against external shocks. Citizens have an obligation to contribute to the government's revenue through payments of taxes and other required fees, while the government has a reciprocal obligation to manage these resources properly. Transparency in how funds are managed is important to ensure that public funds are spent efficiently and for their intended purposes.

PFM has been defined as the practice of allocating financial resources through political processes to serve different human purposes (Wildavsky 1986); it has also been described as the way governments manage public resources in the short- and medium-term and the impact of these resources on the economy (Andrews 2014). In broad terms, PFM is concerned with the laws, rules, organizations, systems, processes and procedures available to governments to secure and use resources effectively, efficiently and transparently. Sound PFM supports accountability in the management of public resources, which is critical to the achievement of public trust in meeting government policy objectives.

In summary, a PFM system is similar to a pipe structure through which water (monetary resources) is channelled and managed within the whole government, with the ultimate goal of positively impacting the economy and society.

1.3 GLOBAL TREND OF PFM REFORM

Cambodia launched a Public Financial Management Reform Program (PFMRP) in 2004 with detailed, prioritized and sequenced action plans for public financial management reform. The program is guided by a long-term step-by-step platform approach with the aim to install high standards of management and accountability in the mobilization of government resources.

Historically, one of the catalysts for embarking on public financial management reform stems from "shocks" such as financial or economic crises that pressure governments to focus on reforming their inefficient financial systems for better governance. PFM systems are improved over time: however, as a set of improvements is made, a new set of challenges arise that must be met, which keeps the momentum of the reform process going.

In 1987, New Zealand, which had experienced deficits for the previous two decades, was faced with a currency crisis that led to the need to devalue its currency by 20 per cent, affecting the overall fiscal balance. A new government at the time took radical steps to address the crisis and passed the Public Finance Act 1989, which required the government to produce a proper "corporate" balance sheet, making it the first sovereign government to do so. The 2008 financial crisis led many governments to undertake significant financial management reforms. In Asia, the 1997–98 Asian Financial Crisis prompted countries such as Thailand and Indonesia to accelerate their measures for reforms. For other countries such as Timor-Leste and Afghanistan, the impetus came from a profound political change with an urgent need for reconstruction and development. PFM reforms often require a trigger to establish the political consensus for reforms.

Today, in an increasingly technological age, more detailed analyses of government spending and efficiency in the provision of public services can be easily made available to citizens. They need to be reassured that their governments are exercising an appropriate level of diligence in collecting taxes and non-tax revenues and turning these revenues into meaningful public services. Effective communication can help reinforce the delivery of services and obtain the trust of the public.

However, the last couple of decades have shown that PFM reforms are not always easy to achieve and have met with limited success in many countries. This finding holds regardless of whether PFM reforms were tried in low, middle- or upper-income countries (Asian Development Bank 2001). There is a growing realization that ambitious, large-scale reforms may not always work. On the other hand, pragmatic, targeted reforms, and quite simply, a better sequencing of reforms, might lead to more success. Cambodia fits with this model of long-term, step-by-step reforms.

Theories of Public Financial Management

Two significant theories on PFM have evolved and have relevance to Cambodia's reform efforts: New Public Financial Management (NPFM) and the New Political Economy of PFM. NPFM evolved in response to citizens' demand for more information and refers to reforms introduced in systems, procedures, organizations and laws for obtaining and effectively using public financial resources. Implicit in NPFM is the assumption that private sector management techniques and models are generally superior to traditional public administration approaches. On the other hand, New Political Economy is a relatively new branch of economics that examines non-technical factors of money management.

The new approach to PFM moves away from the traditional annual budgeting process, where the focus is on just one year's revenue and expenditure and introduces multiyear budget planning that addresses emerging needs and demands. Cambodia's approach to its PFM reform followed this global trend of taking the longer-term approach to budget reform. In Cambodia, Stage 1 focused on budget creditability, in line with the early technical approaches to NPFM; Stage 2 focused on financial accountability and, Stage 3 moved into policy-budget linkages. Finally, Stage 4 will focus on performance accountability, a key aspect of NPFM.

Initially, budget reform in Cambodia was about adopting "performance-based budgeting" (PBB) by 2020; however, that direction has changed to "performance-informed budgeting" (PIB) to be implemented by 2025 after the adoption of the new Budget System Reform Strategy. Other countries such as Australia, Sweden and Estonia have already evolved to performance-informed budgeting. In this system, the allocation of resources is indirectly related to proposed future performance and thus responds more directly to strategic and policy-based directions. PIB ensures that performance is taken into consideration but is not a technical procedure linked to budget allocation. On the other hand, PBB needs spending priorities and program performance to be formally integrated into the budget process, leaving little flexibility in changing government policy priorities in the short term.

The New Political Economy of PFM is a way of looking at financial management that focuses on factors of production, including land, labour, capital, entrepreneurship and trade, and examines their relationship with the law and government. Political economists study how economic theories such as capitalism, socialism and communism adopted by a society affect the economic structure of a country in its use of scarce resources. Studies exploring the political economy of PFM reform examine the construction of budgets and the impacts of different actors with conflicting interests and incentives, including private individuals, elites and governmental institutions, all acting as economic vehicles within society.

For political economists, the appropriate focus of attention is not on the individual, but on key social groups. These groups are located throughout the economy, with different interests and different sources of power to their interests. In their models, society is conceptualized as structurally unequal, with certain groups consistently dominating agendas and decision-making over time and across issue areas. Analysis of relative political power becomes a significant focus of attention for development practitioners seeking to promote reform programs, particularly those that seek to significantly redistribute resources among social groups (Hudson and Leftwich 2014).

The political economy shifts the focus to the interaction between structure and agency in different development contexts (Hughes and

Hutchison 2012). One example of this is "problem-driven" political economy analysis, which requires understanding the interactions between structural and institutional constraints and stakeholder interests in any particular reform context, where the activities of stakeholders are primarily determined by certain incentives (World Bank 2014). This approach raises the question of what drives such variation in PFM reform across nations and the extent to which structural factors may explain these variations. The analysis looks at the country's characteristics, including macro-social, economic, fiscal, as well as political variables (World Bank 2017).

The underlying political economy shapes PFM reform policy decisions and helps to explain the successes and failures of individual reform efforts. A more in-depth look at how PFM reform has fared in OECD and ASEAN countries is provided in Chapter 7.

1.4 SCOPE AND STRUCTURE

This book is structured into seven chapters. Chapter 1 outlines the book's objectives and scope, and then provides an overview of PFM and global trends in PFM reforms.

Chapter 2 begins with an overall description of economic development in Cambodia and the PFM Reform Program (PFMRP), including a historical overview of the economy and public financial situation since 1993. The chapter also highlights key achievements, challenges and possible ways forward for the PFMRP. Cross-cutting reform programs, including their impact on the budget process, civil service reform and Decentralization and De-concentration (D&D), are also discussed in this chapter.

Chapter 3 provides a deeper exploration of how PFM reform affects strategic planning and budgeting. It uses the Medium-Term Fiscal Framework and the Medium-Term Budget Framework to put PFM reform in the context of overall planning and budgeting in the RGC.

Chapter 4 examines the various components of PFM in a more detailed manner, including the management of revenues, expenditures, investment and public debt. Furthermore, this chapter also touches on state property management, public procurement, accounting systems, the financial management information system and auditing.

Chapter 5 focuses on tools for PFM system assessment, including Public Expenditure and Financial Accountability Framework (PEFA), Open Budget Survey (OBS), Public Investment Management Assessment (PIMA) and Tax Administration Diagnostic Assessment Tool (TADAT).

Chapter 6 provides case studies of the PFMRP's implementation at the Ministry of Education, Youth and Sport, the Ministry of Rural Development and at Subnational Administration.

Chapter 7 examines the PFM experiences of selected ASEAN and OECD countries, including Thailand, Vietnam, the Philippines, Malaysia, Indonesia, New Zealand, France, Australia, Sweden and Estonia. The chapter also describes lessons that are useful for building a robust PFM system in Cambodia.

NOTES
1. Bilateral aid is the assistance given by a government directly to the government of another country.
2. Multilateral aid is delivered through international institutions such as the various agencies in the United Nations, World Bank and Asian Development Bank. The OECD estimates that in 2018 around 73.3 per cent of international assistance was channelled through multilateral institutions.

CHAPTER TWO

Overview of Cambodian Economy and PFM Reform Program

2.1 HISTORICAL OVERVIEW OF THE CAMBODIAN ECONOMY

Since its independence from France in 1953, Cambodia has had an unfortunate history of sudden regime changes that led to repeated changes in economic policies. During the Sangkum Reastr Niyum Regime (1953–70) period, the government placed importance on the agricultural sector, promoting policies to increase rice production yields by adopting innovative irrigation systems. The industrial sector benefited from foreign economic assistance from Czechoslovakia, Japan, Australia, China, France and the Soviet Union, including the production of textiles, glass, tires, rubber and sugar, while the government also expanded transportation and communication networks.

During the Khmer Republic Regime (1970–75) the economy was called the "Wartime Economy". The war that engulfed the rest of Indochina spread to Cambodia in April 1970. Wartime conditions had a major impact on the country's economy. Production and export of all commodities significantly dropped as insecurity spread throughout the countryside. Despite the government's effort to liberalize the economy to save the nation from economic disaster by implementing a comprehensive program of reforms, maintaining a policy of strict political neutrality, and accepting foreign assistance, political instability has plunged the country into civil war.

During the Democratic Kampuchea Regime, more commonly known as the Khmer Rouge Regime (1975–79), the economic and financial systems were devastated. This regime overhauled the social and economic system; there was no currency, no bank or any monetary transactions, and no schools. The regime tried to build the economy on the agricultural sector is supported by local small enterprises and handicrafts. Part of its economic policy was to use revenues from agriculture to support the development of the industrial sector, which it later used to support the agricultural sector. However, this approach turned out to be a huge failure for the country, resulting in starvation and the death of millions of people.

In January 1979, the formation of the People's Republic of Kampuchea (PRK) marked a new stage in the country's rehabilitation and reconstruction. Cambodia employed a Soviet-style planned economy throughout the 1980s. The economic system was divided into three areas: (1) the "State Economy" covering large-scale agricultural production, all industrial production, communications, transport networks, and foreign trade within a managed and facilitated economic transaction environment; (2) the "Collective Economy" covering agricultural rehabilitation and development, forestry and handicraft, and any task of collective purchase and sale; and (3) the "Family-run Economy" covering the home economy of peasants, retail businesses, individual artisans, handicraft repair shops and small trade (Slocomb 2010).

Since the early 1990s, Cambodia has gradually moved away from a planned economy towards a market-oriented one. It increased its involvement in regional and global integration activities by becoming a member of ASEAN in 1999 and the WTO in 2004. The private sector was designated as the main driver of economic growth. State-owned Enterprises (SOEs) were privatized to mitigate their debt burden on the government and foreign direct investment (FDI) was attracted to create jobs and boost exports.

According to the World Bank's 1999 public expenditure review report,[1] since 1993 Cambodia had made remarkable progress in stabilizing the economy, restoring economic growth, and undertaking policy reforms that transformed the economy into a market-oriented one. In particular, inflation, which averaged 140 per cent per annum during the early 1990s, was reduced to single digits in 1995. However, after 1996, despite the government's efforts, the implementation of critical fiscal and structural reforms stalled due to various factors, especially external ones.

In 1997, the Asian Financial Crisis, originating in Thailand, had a severe negative impact on the wider regional economy. Cambodia was also affected but relatively less harmed compared to other countries as it was a dollarized economy, and its financial sector was underdeveloped. However, the subsequent Global Financial Crisis in 2008–9 negatively impacted Cambodia's growth performance. This was primarily due to the drop in demand for garment exports, which is the country's dominant export, resulting in significant job losses before recovering in the following years.

Despite these tribulations and setbacks, Cambodia is now one of the fast-growing economies in the world with an average annual GDP growth rate of 7 per cent during 2009–19. Cambodia graduated from low-income country status and became a lower middle-income country in 2015. The inflation rate was also stable, averaging around 2.8 per cent during the same period. As shown in Table 2.1, the country's per capita income reached US$1,643 in 2019 (World Bank 2021). As a result of this high growth performance, Cambodia's poverty rate has also significantly declined, from 53.2 per cent in 2004 to just 12.9 per cent in 2018. Per capita GDP has increased by more than sixfold and exports were 45 times during the same period. According to its Industrial Development Policy (IDP), Cambodia aspires to become an upper-middle-income country by 2030 and a high-income country by 2050, and various policy measures have been set out to achieve this ambitious goal. However, the COVID-19 pandemic

TABLE 2.1
Economic Development, 1993–2019

	1993	2004	2019
Economic status	low income	low income	lower middle income
Gross domestic product	US$2.5 billion	US$5.3 billion	US$27.1 billion
GDP per capita	US$254	US$408	US$1,643
Total trade volume	US$755 million	US$5,991 million	US$35,104 million
Exports	US$284 million	US$2,798 million	US$14,825 million
Domestic revenue	US$72.5 million	US$555 million	US$5,424 million
Poverty rate	–	53.2%	12.9%

Source: World Bank, *World Development Indicators* Online and data on poverty rate is from the National Institute of Statistics (Cambodia Socio-Economic Survey 2020).

has posed challenges to the country's growth performance. It was later exacerbated by the Russia-Ukraine war, raising energy prices and adding more uncertainty to the world and Cambodian economy.

2.2 PUBLIC FINANCE IN CAMBODIA

Cambodia had its first general election in May 1993 after the conclusion of the Paris Peace Accord, putting an end to almost two decades of internal conflicts. After the election, a new government was formed and with support from the international community, it began formulating a comprehensive macroeconomic and structural reform program. Major customs reforms were instituted, and a taxation structure was established. Non-tax revenues began to increasingly flow into the government coffer rather than being appropriated by private agents. The bulk of revenues was generated by taxes on international trade and turnover taxes, with domestic excise accounting for a relatively small share.

Before the introduction of the PFM in late 2004, the fiscal situation in Cambodia was in distress. As shown in Table 2.2, the current expenditures accounted for over half of total expenditure and the government consistently incurred a current fiscal deficit. This deficit was financed largely by foreign aid receipts from 1993 to 1997. Domestic public investment was therefore completely financed by foreign savings. A significant majority of recurrent expenditure was on military spending and salary for government officials, with some donor-financed current expenditures providing for basic non-wage operating expenses.

During 1997–98, fiscal performance largely repeated the delicate pattern of the preceding years: civilian non-wage operating expenditures were compressed significantly to sustain macroeconomic stability in response to a revenue shortfall and an overrun in defence and security outlays. According to the World Bank's expenditure review in 1999, budgetary developments in 1998 were particularly problematic. The government had borrowed KHR82 billion (or 0.8 per cent of GDP) from the National Bank of Cambodia (NBC) to pay salary arrears, integrate Khmer Rouge defectors, and finance part of the election costs—after having avoided bank financing of the budget deficit since 1994.

TABLE 2.2
Fiscal Performance, 1993–2002 (KHR billion)

	1993	1994	1995	1996	1997	1998	1999	2000	2001	2002
Total revenue	290	590	643	749	881	943	1,338	1,442	1,561	1,834
Total expenditure	608	1,009	1,206	1,441	1,260	1,571	1,927	2,119	2,367	2,682
Current expenditure	373	674	695	813	808	941	1,119	1,223	1,391	1,620
Current balance	–83	–85	–59	–103	61	–32	205	188	160	189
Overall fiscal balance	–318	–419	–563	–692	–379	–628	–589	–677	–806	–848
Overall fiscal balance (including grants)		–69	–105	–113	–38	–286	–247	–293	–410	–369

Note: The exchange rate between the US dollar and Khmer riel fluctuates at around US$1 = KHR4,000.
Source: United Nations Development Program, *Pro-Poor Fiscal Policy in Cambodia*, p. 2. Data provided by the IMF Country Office, Cambodia.

TABLE 2.3
Public Finance

	2000	2005	2010	2015	2017	2018	2019	2020 (est.)
Total revenue (% GDP)	11.2	10.3	17.0	19.6	21.6	23.7	26.8	24.5
Total expenditure (% GDP)	16.4	13.7	19.9	20.9	22.4	23.0	23.8	28.0
Public external debt (% GDP)	67.6*	33.9	28.7	31.2	30.0	28.4	28.2	35.2

Note: *This figure includes the bilateral debt with the Russian Federation and the United States and reflects the impact of completing rescheduling agreements on Naples terms with these creditors in mid-2003.
Source: IMF, Article IV (2002, 2007, 2012, 2022).

The PFM reform program started in late 2004 and through the revenue mobilization strategy, the government revenue collection has increased drastically. During the first stage of PFM reform, Stage 1 (2005–8), which is budget credibility, it addressed the chronic cash shortage by focusing on revenue mobilization. As shown in Table 2.3, the share of total revenue to GDP has increased significantly, from only 10.3 per cent in 2005 to 17 per cent in 2010, and 26.8 per cent in 2019. As a result, the total expenditure has also increased from only 13.7 per cent in 2005 to 19.9 per cent in 2010 and 23.8 per cent in 2019. Public debt remains low by regional standards, with a low risk of distress, at 28.2 per cent of GDP in 2019. In 2020, due to the expanded expenditure to respond to COVID-19, the Cambodian government has boosted its social program to address the vulnerable group and keep affected businesses afloat. As a result, the share of public debt to GDP has increased to 35.2 per cent. However, this remains at low risk of debt stress despite an increase in both debt disbursements and public-private partnerships (PPPs) to finance needed infrastructure investment (International Monetary Fund 2002, 2007, 2012, 2022).

According to Cambodian public debt management, the government adheres to four key principles for borrowing: (1) keep within the affordability levels of the budget and economy; (2) obtain excellent preferential terms; (3) focus on priority sectors to support sustainable economic growth and increase economic productivity, particularly infrastructure; and (4) be sure loans have high transparency, accountability, efficiency and effectiveness. In 1994, the share of government debt to GDP reached 69.7 per cent (US$1,909 million); however, in 2019, this number declined significantly to less than 30 per cent in 2019.[2]

2.3 PFM REFORM PROGRAM IN CAMBODIA
2.3.1 Overview

PFM Reform Program (PFMRP) was launched under the chairmanship of Samdech Akka Moha Sena Padey Techo Hun Sen, Prime Minister of the Kingdom of Cambodia on 5 December 2004. The PFMRP is one of the key reform agendas of the Royal Government of Cambodia (RGC) aimed at strengthening good governance, a core component of the Rectangular Strategy, which is Cambodia's overall approach to economic growth and national development. With an ambitious vision and realistic plan, Cambodia's PFM system was created through a gradual change from an input-based and centralized budget system towards a performance-based and decentralized budget system. This PFM system has been envisioned to lead to: (1) integrity of budget discipline, (2) increased efficiency of the budget in both allocation and operation, and (3) greater effectiveness of public service delivery.

The reform was well thought out and embraced a gradual and well-sequenced implementation through a "platform approach" with four stages, or platforms.[3] Stage 1 (2005–8) focused on achieving budget credibility through increased revenue mobilization and predictable overall budget execution. Its success has resulted in macroeconomic stability and expanded fiscal space for the government. Stage 2 (2009–15) aimed at achieving basic budget accountability in government agencies. The Financial Management Information System (FMIS) was introduced, along with a modern chart of accounts based on International Public Sector Accounting Standards (IPSAS) and new budget classifications. Stage 3 (2016–20) focused on linking budget allocations with each ministry's policies and the government's overall policies. The PFM Reform Steering Committee (PFMR-SC) decided to extend the implementation of Stage 3 by two years into 2022. This extension will further build a robust foundation for Stage 4, performance accountability which is expected to start in 2023.

2.3.2 Rationale for PFM Reform

Unlike other countries, Cambodia is highly dollarized. In the mid-1980s, the United Nations (UN) sent humanitarian and emergency aid to Cambodia. International non-government organizations were allowed to set up in the country, and remittances from abroad were allowed to flow in. Cambodians who fled the country to refugee camps in Thailand during the Khmer Rouge Regime returned home in 1985 and brought large amounts of cash in Thai baht and US dollars.

Starting from 1991, the dollarization process gained momentum as a result of three major factors. First, the United Nations Transitional Authority in Cambodia (UNTAC) facilitated the country's first democratic election following the Paris Peace Agreement by injecting approximately

US$2 billion into the country for its operation. These funds accounted for over 80 per cent of the country's GDP at that time. Second, the inflows of official development assistance (ODA) and FDIs into the country in the following years had been primarily in US dollars. And finally, the general acceptance of foreign currencies by the population was largely due to the lack of confidence in the domestic currency, the Khmer riel.

This high dollarization rate persisted despite Cambodia's significant political and macroeconomic stability. While dollarization also has its merits such as confidence for FDI firms to invest in the country to support growth, it also limits the ability of the National Bank of Cambodia to effectively perform its monetary policy. The government's ability to raise funds through the bond market can only be done in domestic currency (KHR) and this accounts for approximately only 20 per cent of the total money in circulation.

In the late 1990s, the medium-term prospects remained bleak for the domestic currency unless the government swiftly took decisive actions to address the interrelated fiscal and governance problems. The RGC, in its Second Mandate, 1998–2003, demonstrated an awareness of this need by reaffirming a commitment to implement the necessary fiscal and structural reforms and creating the PFM Reform Program.

In the subsequent mandates, the RGC has continued its strong commitment to PFM reform, seeking to develop and strengthen fiscal and monetary policies, address and improve the accessibility of public services to the poor, strengthen macroeconomic stability, alleviate poverty, and support inclusive economic growth.

2.3.3 PFM Institutional Arrangement

The Royal Decree 1444 promulgated in 2013, stipulates that the Economic and Financial Policy Committee (EFPC) is the governing body that oversees the preparation, implementation, monitoring and evaluation of economic and financial policies. Its purview includes the PFMRP as well as financial sector development, private sector development, and the coordination with development partners (DPs) with regard to public financial reforms. The EFPC oversees PFMRP through the PFMR-SC, which is chaired by the Minister of Economy and Finance and includes members from the National

Bank of Cambodia, Ministers, Secretaries and Under-Secretaries of State and management level from relevant line ministries (LMs). It meets with the Development Partners Committee (DPC) quarterly and annually as part of the PFM Technical Working Group (PFM-TWG) to review reform progress and determine its future direction. All active donors in the PFM sector are coordinated by a lead development partner[4] who serves as a facilitator in aligning and harmonizing all donors' support to achieve PFMRP progress and development results. The PFMR-SC oversees the progress of PFMRP implementation and is responsible for guiding implementation throughout the relevant units of the Ministry of Economy and Finance and other line ministries.

The General Secretariat of the PFM Reform Steering Committee (GSC) serves the PFM-SC and provides day-to-day operational support to both the PFM Steering Commission in MEF (MEF-RC) and PFM Technical Working Groups (PFM-TWG) in LMs. GSC works closely with the PFM-TWGs and facilitates discussions on PFM Roadmap, PFM-related matters and issues, financing agreements, and the Quarterly and Annual PFM Report. GSC has seven crucial roles and responsibilities (Figure 2.1), including:

(1) Design policies, strategies, and consolidated action plan (CAP). The CAP framework was formulated for each stage of the PFMRP. All implementing agencies within MEF and LMs have to prepare action plans under this framework.
(2) As part of preparing quarterly and annual reports, GSC raises pending issues or challenges and proposes solutions to PFMR-RC and PFMR-SC or PFM-TWG during the quarterly and annual meetings.
(3) Under the CAP framework, GCS works with MEF's general departments to formulate the General Departmental Action Plan (GDAP) and coordinate with LMs to prepare Ministerial Action Plan (MAP).
(4) Formulate a budget to support the implementation of PFMRP.
(5) Monitor and evaluate the PFMRP implementation progress and prepare quarterly and annual reports for PFM-RC, PFMSC and PFM-TWG.
(6) Coordinate with other cross-cutting reform programs, including Public Administrative Reform and D&D Reform, to ensure reform alignment.
(7) Promote PFMRP to all stakeholders to increase awareness of the reform program.

FIGURE 2.1
Roles and Responsibilities of GSC

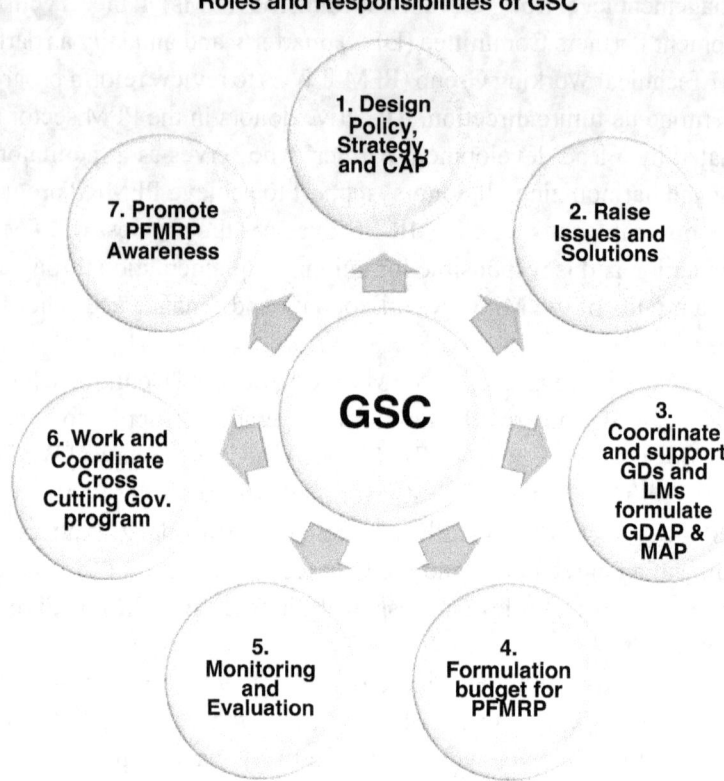

Source: Authors' illustration.

2.4 PFM AND DEVELOPMENT PARTNERS' COOPERATION

Informed by international good practices, the RGC puts a focus on ownership, partnership and results in its development of cooperation strategies. These strategies aim to guide RGC's effort to mobilize and manage the flow of DPs' resources to support Cambodia's development. The strategies are tailored to the Cambodian development context and specify tools and mechanisms for RGC agencies to advance partnerships with DPs. The PFM Reform Program has received both financial and technical assistance from development partners through various modes.

In 2006, the RGC and its development partners jointly adopted the Paris Declaration to enhance aid effectiveness. The adoption gave rise to aid-effectiveness principles and informed cooperation practices, namely, the multi-donor trust fund; European Union; Asian Development Bank; United Nations Children's Fund; International Monetary Fund; and bilateral support.

Multi-Donor Trust Fund

Coordinated by the World Bank, a multi-donor trust fund was created in 2005 in line with the aid-effectiveness principles to provide technical and financial support to PFMRP. This aid source harmonized funding from the European Union, the Swedish International Development Cooperation Agency (SIDA), the Department for International Development (DFID) of the United Kingdom, and the Australian Department of Foreign Affairs and Trade (DFAT). This multi-donor trust fund mechanism supported PFM reform through two projects until 2017, the last project being the Public Financial Management Modernization Project. This project aimed to enhance public financial management by strengthening revenue mobilization, and budget execution processes through the implementation of the FMIS. This effort had a period of four years and a total cost of US$18 million. Specifically, this project had several beneficial effects:

- improved timeliness in compiling financial data and reporting;
- improved timeliness in payment processing at the General Department of National Treasury (GDNT);
- more timely closure of financial accounts at the end of the fiscal year;
- more information available on non-tax revenue sources;
- increased revenues from property tax;
- improved budget classification through the implementation of a uniform account code structure;
- financial statements that include a disclosure of the accounting standards used as the basis for their preparation and the accounting policies that were followed;

- FMIS is implemented at MEF and Capital/Provincial Treasuries (PTs);
- budget control and execution modules implemented; and
- revenue mobilization action plans developed, and their implementation monitored.

However, support from the trust fund did not stop there, and in total thirteen development partners coordinated their assistance to great success during that period.

European Union (EU)

The European Development Cooperation Strategy for Cambodia 2014–19 reflected the EU Member States and Switzerland's plan to work in partnership with the RGC and others to ensure greater coherence, predictability, impact and transparency of European development assistance to Cambodia. Strengthening national governance through the implementation of institutional reforms is at the core of European efforts. With this objective, the European Joint Strategy stated that the PFMRP remains essential to finance vast development needs without jeopardizing fiscal sustainability. Therefore, European partners are committed to supporting the PFMRP aimed at improving the efficiency and effectiveness of Cambodia's public financial management system according to international standards, through enhancing budget credibility and transparency, enhancing financial accountability through introducing the FMIS and strengthening links between planning, budgeting and results.

Since 2015 the grant modality has been changed from program support to budget support implemented by the EU with a joint program with the Swedish International Development Cooperation Agency (SIDA). The EU provided budget support to the Public Financial Management Reform Program Stage 3 (2016–20). The overall objectives of the program were to enhance domestic revenue mobilization, make improvements in the effective use of resources, and to better align expenditures with national priorities to improve the government's service delivery and spur economic growth. Specifically, it aimed at improving: (1) institutional capacity to implement reform, (2) national statistics for better fiscal planning,

(3) national budget comprehensiveness and transparency, (4) policy-based budgeting, (5) predictability and control in national budget execution, (6) accounting, recording and reporting, (7) external scrutiny and audit of the national budget, and (8) public accountability.

On 23 May 2019, a new Financing Agreement was signed, covering the period 2019–20 with additional budget support of €22 million (€14 million of direct budget support and €8 million in technical assistance), to enable the continuation of the EU support to the PFM reform for two years. The second top-up budget support for 2019–20 was to improve Government's service delivery and promote economic growth.

Asian Development Bank (ADB)

The ADB has provided both financial assistance linked to policy compliance and general technical assistance to the PFMRP. It offered grants to implement a sector-wide approach to strengthen rural PFM systems. The ADB has also provided US$20 million in concessional loans to support the de-concentration and capacity-building of PFMRP in eight-line ministries since 2017.

The Strengthening Public Financial Management Program (SPFMP) under an ADB loan agreement supported the implementation of Stage 3 of the government's four-stage PFMRP to improve budget-policy linkages. The SPFMP particularly supports actions and initiatives to strengthen the policy and regulatory framework for expenditure and revenue management, the capacity of selected line ministries to implement budgeting and expenditure management reforms, and the capacity of the external audit function. The first two outcomes are the responsibility of the Ministry of Economy and Finance (MEF) with the General Secretariat of the PFM Reform Steering Committee (GSC) taking responsibility as the program director. The audit capacity outcome is the responsibility of the National Audit Authority (NAA) as the "Implementing Agency" (IA). The SPFMP funding totalled US$30 million.

United Nations Children's Fund (UNICEF)

UNICEF supports the implementation of the consolidated training manual for Budget Strategic Plans (BSP), program-based budgeting

(PBB) and budget execution, the establishment of an automated budget formulation system, and systematization of more regular dialogue and comprehensive feedback between the MEF budget department and key social sector ministries. The rationale for UNICEF support was that it is aimed at strengthening budget allocation, thereby allowing more children and adolescents in Cambodia, especially the most deprived to benefit from more effective social services and a child-sensitive social protection system.

International Monetary Fund (IMF)

The IMF has financed two technical advisors to MEF in the fields of accounting, budget execution and macroeconomic analysis. Additionally, IMF's Fiscal Affairs Department and Technical Assistance Office in Thailand have provided technical assistance to monitor and advise on the progress of the FMIS Phase II roll-out and to define the scope of the IMF's support related to this initiative.

Bilateral Support

In addition to the multi-donor trust fund, some development partners have also supported PFMRP through additional bilateral technical assistance. For example, the Japan International Cooperation Agency (JICA) supports tax administration, customs policy and customs administration, public investment policy, and aid management.

2.5 REFORM APPROACH

The PFMRP is designed to be implemented in four successive stages, also called platform approach: (1) budget credibility; (2) financial accountability; (3) budget-policy linkages; and (4) performance accountability.

- *Platform 1: Budget Credibility* focused on developing a reliable budget and delivering predictable resources. It includes establishing and strengthening revenue collection, developing fiscal space, improving revenue forecasting and macro-fiscal modelling, establishing cash management procedures, implementing procurement reform, and

putting in place a debt management strategy with modern management tools.
- *Platform 2: Financial Accountability* aimed at providing financial information promptly, mainly through FMIS implementation and the improvement of internal controls to hold managers accountable. It also included: implementing a modern chart of accounts based on IPSAS standards; developing a new budget classification method; a transaction coding structure and a set of accounting rules; clarifying lines of responsibilities through a clear budget entity structure linked to a responsibility/expenditure assignment; and developing a reporting structure, including financial statements that comply with international standards.
- *Platform 3: Budget-Policy Linkage* emphasizes improving the linkages between economic planning and economic policy priorities—as reflected in the National Sustainable Development Plan (NSDP)—and budget planning. It includes developing a hierarchy of medium-term programming tools and implementing program budgeting with some elements of fiscal decentralization.
- *Platform 4: Performance-Based Management* intends to deliver broad accountability through a stronger linkage between PFM processes and performance-based management and budgeting.

Every stage of the PFM reform corresponds to a Consolidated Action Plan (CAP). The Consolidated Action Plan 3 (CAP 3) guided and monitored the reform implementation for the period 2016–20 on budget-policy linkages. The PFMRP Platform 3 included the consolidation of the financial accountability platform by expanding the FMIS to line ministries and introducing a systemic link between budget preparation and sector policy priorities. Despite many achievements in Platform 3, the RGC had decided to extend CAP 3 for two more years (through 2022) based on the review of CAP 3 implementation. This decision aimed to further strengthen the foundation achieved in Platform 3 before stepping into Platform 4, which is expected to be implemented between 2023 and 2027. These two years' implementation will build the necessary prerequisites for Performance-Informed Budgeting in all government agencies.

2.6 ACHIEVEMENTS, CHALLENGES AND WAYS FORWARD

2.6.1 Achievements

Through the efforts of the RGC in cooperation with its development partners in more than fifteen years of reform, Cambodian PFM systems have been substantially strengthened. First, a solid foundation for budget credibility has been built through the strengthening of revenue mobilization mechanisms, more effective public spending, and better management of public debts. This allows the RGC to appropriately control budget deficits, improve budget efficiency (both allocation and operational efficiency) and eliminate prolonged spending arrears.

Domestic revenue gradually increased from only 8.5 per cent of GDP in 2004 to 24.9 per cent in 2019.[5] Prudent fiscal management led to low public debt ratios (21.3 per cent of GDP at the end of 2019).[6] This rise in revenue has enabled the RGC to substantially increase expenditure and domestic investment to improve the quality and coverage of public services, bringing them closer to people.

Building a solid PFM system to strengthen budget credibility also enabled the government to effectively respond to crises, particularly the COVID-19 pandemic, through the good performance of revenue collection and efficiency of expenditure management.[7] Cambodia's budget has become more independent and has stronger governmental ownership, particularly between 2013 and 2017, even as the government's total expenditure doubled.

Second, financial accountability has been improved with the launch of the Financial Management Information System (FMIS). FMIS helps enhance internal audit function in line ministries as well as improve the procedures, rules, and regulations of financial management. The FMIS is currently functioning within the Ministry of Economy and Finance and is used by all line ministries. In the future, FMIS will become the core platform for budget execution and financial accountability at all levels, including financial control, cash management and program implementation.

Third, budget and policy linkages have been strengthened through the implementation of complete program budgeting in all line ministries and all capital-provincial level administrations. In this effort, budget preparations and negotiations have been improved to reflect the RGC's key priorities.

Fourth, fiscal transparency has been improved. This is reflected in the dissemination of budget information through its disclosure at every stage of the budget cycle, from the preparation of the macroeconomic framework and drafting of the budget law to the budget approval process and execution.

Last, and most important of all, is that the RCG has achieved high economic growth while ensuring more equitable distribution and overall macroeconomic stability. Public financial management is not only about collecting revenue to meet expenditures but also about effective management and allocation of scarce public resources to spur economic growth and development. The government has carefully set appropriate revenue collection targets while maintaining a favourable environment for investment and business activities.

At the same time, the government should also consider social equity by easing the tax burden on low-income citizens while increasing expenditures for priority sectors that support economic growth and ensuring budget sustainability. The economic growth of around 7 per cent per annum, stable macroeconomic conditions of low inflation, stable exchange rates and remarkable improvement of PFM has provided opportunities for new job creation and increased earnings. The average monthly salary for civil servants and the armed forces steadily increased from approximately KHR340,000 (US$85) in 2013 to more than KHR1 million (US$250) in 2018. Pension and other benefits for retirees have also been gradually increased as part of National Social Protection policies. Similarly, for the private sector, the minimum wage in the garment industry has gradually increased, from only US$80 in 2013 to US$170 per month in 2018.[8]

In addition, the RGC has enforced many policies to address the hardship and concerns of the people at the national and subnational levels. These include: eliminating motorbike driving licence fees; providing tax exemption on motorbike and tricycle vehicles with engine capacity below 150 CC; providing a birth certificate, marriage certificate and national identity card free of charge; lowering electricity and water costs; abolishing the "estimated tax regime"; raising the minimum threshold of salary tax;

eliminating stamp duties on properties transfer among relatives; exempting levies for petty sellers; allowing the transfer of ownership and titles of stalls in public markets; removing taxes on slaughterhouses; and breaking up geographic monopolies. These measures have benefited the public in general, especially those in low-income segments.

2.6.2 Challenges

However, PFMRP implementation has not been without challenges. Since 2005, the first year of implementation, key challenges have included:

- *Limited understanding of PFM reform among line ministries and institutions.* Line ministries and institutions perceived PFM reform as routine work under the responsibility of finance departments, while it is the reform program of the government.
- *Lack of emphasis on Business Process Reengineering (BPR).* The PFMRP did not place enough emphasis on BPR[9] (referred to in Cambodia as "business process streamlining") to support changes in institutional structures and work responsibilities and assign newly trained officials to the right jobs to assure the sustainable implementation of a new system.
- *The coordination of needs and resources was underestimated.* When PFMRP was rolled out to all line ministries, the discussion was focused on administrative work and the message of the PFM reform agenda to all relevant agencies. However, little emphasis was placed on the resources required to achieve the goal.
- *Ministries have operated in silos.* This is a historical legacy since the new government was set up in the first half of the 1990s. Each ministry was established through a Royal Decree and thus had colossal autonomy. Cambodia has a very centralized, French-based system with lots of *ex ante* approvals for financial management, limiting the autonomy of LMs.
- In some cases, *finding technical solutions tailored to Cambodia has been challenging for MEF and line ministries.* In particular, engaging and rolling out the FMIS system, creating the mechanisms to accommodate the Treasury Single Account, and establishing medium- and long-term

strategic budget planning that links with strategic documents (such as the Rectangular Strategy) have been challenging due to the limited technical capacity of the staff on the ground.
- *Significant capacity constraint to implement PFMRP.* It is quite evident that concerted capacity development and training programs must accompany the PFM reforms. Despite all the training, their efficiency and effectiveness remain in question, particularly in determining how to best utilize trained officials. This experience also resonates with other countries in the region. Chapter 7 will describe how Indonesia, Malaysia, Thailand and Vietnam have faced problems with the capacity to absorb the PFM Reforms, particularly at the lower levels of government.

2.6.3 Ways Forward

Ensuring that PFM systems positively impact the quality-of-service delivery requires more progress, at both the central and sectoral levels. This includes improving the allocation and execution of public resources while achieving increased efficiency. These issues require attention for PFM reform to be fully successful:

- *Revenue sustainability:* Revenue mobilization has delivered good results, but it is not yet sustainable. Even though tax collection has almost reached its potential, the institutional structure for managing revenue is not robust. Moreover, non-tax revenue collection remains low. The institutional aspects of tax and non-tax revenue management mechanisms have room for further improvement, and this will form a significant part of Stage 4 of the reforms.
- *FMIS adoption and functionality:* Although the FMIS is a core system of financial accountability, it has yet to become fully functional. Specifically, the automation of the production of comprehensive reports and budget execution is not yet implementable, with many still done manually. To move all business processes to the FMIS system, further capacity building for staff on the ground and the strong commitment of leadership to support this effort are required.[10]
- *Quality of program budgeting and budget entities system:* Program budgeting and the budget entities' system have been rolled out to all

line ministries and capital-provincial administrations. Yet, the quality of programs is not satisfactory in terms of substance, structure and performance information. Furthermore, some line ministries have based their programs on administrative structures, rather than linking the program to policy objectives and to the delivery of program outcomes. This is because implementing programs based on administrative structures is easier to achieve and presents less disruption to the ministries. At the same time, some line ministries continue to centrally manage their budgets without providing autonomy in spending, allocations, or policy dialogue and feedback.

- *Budget execution procedures:* The procedures for budget execution have been streamlined, but they are not yet able to ensure timeliness, compliance and predictability. MEF has revised its procedures, leaving the line ministries to streamline their respective internal procedures to improve effectiveness and transparency.
- *State property management:* State property management, which is a part of public resource management, remains a challenge. This is mainly due to the state property using definitions that were not updated on the state property lists because of conflicts of interest. The management of state property and both financial and non-financial assets require more attention as other reform areas are advancing well.[11]
- *Institutionalization of Medium-Term Fiscal Framework (MTFF) and Medium-Term Budget Framework (MTBF):* MTFF was formulated but delayed due to the uncertainty of the economy, resulting from COVID-19 pandemic and MTBF was piloted in 2019 for the budget year 2020–22, to improve the quality of the Budget Strategic Plan (BSP). However, they will need further efforts if the system is ever institutionalized.
- *Decentralization:* While the budget formulation is based on a program, the organizational structure needs to modernize by delegating more authority to the budget entities. In this context, managers are primarily accountable for performance or results. Financial accountability for such performance could be enhanced and monitored through strengthening roles of internal audit and inspection at the line ministries.

To address the above challenges and to pave a concrete road map for a way forward, the RGC adopted 5 strategies (Figure 2.2), including

FIGURE 2.2
Five Strategies under PFMRP

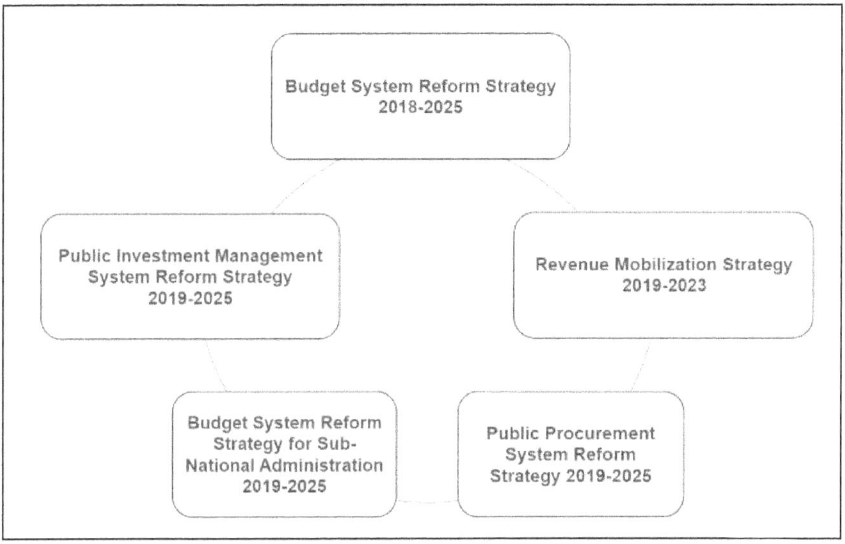

- Budget System Reform Strategy 2018-2025
- Public Investment Management System Reform Strategy 2019-2025
- Revenue Mobilization Strategy 2019-2023
- Budget System Reform Strategy for Sub-National Administration 2019-2025
- Public Procurement System Reform Strategy 2019-2025

Source: Authors' illustration.

Budget System Reform Strategy 2018–25 which is the main strategy and four others such as Revenue Mobilization Strategy 2019–23, Public Investment Management System Reform Strategy 2019–25, Budget System Reform Strategy for Subnational Administration 2019–25, and Public Procurement System Reform Strategy 2019—25 have to go in parallel in order to achieve the objective set in the main strategy. Each strategy, setting clear objectives and targets, will direct reform actions in the forthcoming medium term.

Budget System Reform Strategy (2018–25)

The fundamental objective of this strategy is to move to a performance-informed budget process, following the strategic direction of policy budget linkages and performance accountability by 2025. Under this system, the budget is prepared based on a program with a clear performance framework. The budget preparation process will be made more open and transparent and budget reviews by the legislative body will be further enhanced.

Revenue Mobilization Strategy (2019–23)

Tax and non-tax revenue policies and administration will be modernized to ensure efficient and effective revenue collection, improve the investment environment, strengthen competitiveness, and promote national economic diversification. The strategic objectives are to increase recurrent revenue collection by at least 0.3 percentage point of GDP per annum and to promote the quality of services and productivity of all types of services in tax and non-tax revenue administrations. The strategic preparation approach focuses on (1) ensuring sustainable economic growth, (2) maintaining revenue sustainability at an optimal level, (3) ensuring fairness in the implementation of tax and non-tax policies as well as the revenue collection, and (4) ensuring social equity in easing the tax burden for low-income people and enhancing people's welfare and environmental protection.

Public Investment Management System Reform Strategy (2019–25)

The RGC has to develop a national public investment management system that ensures responsiveness, efficiency, effectiveness, transparency, and accountability. Furthermore, it must sustainably allocate and use public resources in line with international best practices and Cambodia's actual context. Accelerating economic diversification and strengthening competitiveness are the basis for inclusive and sustainable economic growth and they will help Cambodia achieve its vision of becoming an upper-middle-income country by 2030 and a high-income nation by 2050.

Budget System Reform Strategy for Subnational Administration (2019–25)

The objective of this strategy is to strengthen the implementation of full-fledged program budgeting and to build foundations for the implementation of performance-informed budgeting to ensure the linkage of budget to policy. In particular, the policy objective is that subnational administration units align with the national policy priorities. The annual budget plan requires the assurance of consistency with the BSP while opening to wider participation from involved parties. Meanwhile, the effectiveness of budget allocation and execution will be enhanced through the improvement and simplification of the expenditure procedures, particularly delegating discretion and accountability to each subnational administration.

Public Procurement Reform Strategy (2019–25)

The strategy focuses on increasing the threshold for deciding on procurement implementation by the procuring entities. The increase is based on the procurement system's evaluation results. Concerning procurement decentralization, MEF will transfer procurement functions to the budget controller team attached to LMs while strengthening reporting mechanisms and procurement audits and sanctions.

2.7 PFMRP IMPACT ON THE CAMBODIAN BUDGET SYSTEM

2.7.1 Overview of Budget System

Most governments have difficulty gaining public trust in government budgets, particularly in using budgets as the policy tool to serve citizens efficiently and effectively. Even some more developed countries with sophisticated PFM systems, the latest information technology, stronger institutions and better human resources still face challenges in linking budget to policy, action or performance. Every country is likely to adopt different approaches to budget management reform, but they all have a common objective to achieve results and have a decentralized budgeting system. Since 1990, most governments commenced reforming their budget system by incorporating results-based budget formulation. New Zealand, Canada and the United Kingdom have transformed from an inputs and line item-based budget to a performance-based budget.

2.7.2 Strategic Direction of Budget System

The Law on Public Finance System adopted in 2008 paved the way for the budget system reform. It included the introduction of the Budget Strategic Plan (BSP) and the piloting of program budgeting. In June 2013, the RGC approved the "Concept Note for Strategic Direction of Cambodia's Budget System Reform 2013–2020" to guide the implementation of Stage 3 of the PFMRP. This concept note remains a key document that directs budget system reforms.

The "Concept Note for Strategic Direction of Cambodia's Budget System Reform 2013–2020" sets out the objectives of gradual changes from an input-based and centralized budget system towards a performance-based and decentralized budget system by 2020. With this goal, the concept note sets out the objectives and scope of the reforms under the budget cycle framework: budget formulation, approval, execution and performance monitoring and evaluation. Currently, the objectives and scope related to the first three stages are generally being met in financial system reform. However, there are not many activities yet relating to performance monitoring and evaluation, an objective of PFMRP Stage 4.

The piloting of full-fledged program budgeting in some LMs over the past three years has provided the RGC with a better understanding of the challenges in implementing performance budgeting (PB). The management and senior officials of MEF undertook study visits to some selected countries to gain insights into the application of performance budgeting. The knowledge gained from these study visits, coupled with the Program Budgeting Review's findings, leads to an overall conclusion that the strategic direction of budget system reform in Cambodia needs to be adjusted to become more realistic and practical, as budget systems reform will likely face some major challenges. First, the reform agenda was too optimistic; the understanding of reform and the path to achieving it is still limited. Second, the pace of reforms between the national budget system and other related key areas of reform are not in tandem with one another, nor are they interlinked. Third, human capital and institutional capacity development do not match the goals of reform, and developing them will take a longer timeframe, more resources and a willingness from stakeholders to participate. Finally, the reform process is dynamic as international practices are also constantly evolving.

Other countries' experiences in implementing programs and performance budgeting suggest the necessity of reviewing the objectives and the scope of the reforms to make them more appropriate to current best international practices. At the subnational level, the concept note pointed to the following reform directions:

- Policy objectives and priorities at subnational and national levels need to have more clearly defined roles, authority, and responsibilities for the subnational administration.

- Gradual changes to the budget cycle of the subnational administrations need to be coordinated with the national budget cycle.
- The financial accounting system and management of the subnational administrations need to be aligned with the national level by using the same budget classification, chart of accounts, and reporting formats.

Findings from the study visits suggested that the objectives and scope of the reforms on the subnational budget system remain valid and relevant and do not need any revision.

2.7.3 Performance Budgeting Model

Performance-based budgeting is the allocation of funds based on programmatic results that contribute to organizational goals. Many countries, both developing and developed, have been using different names for and models of performance budgeting systems depending on the country's stage of development, institutional setup, and legislative powers. According to the IMF, performance budgeting can be categorized into three models:

- *Presentational Performance Budgeting:* In this model, performance information is illustrated in budget documents or other government documents. Performance information refers to a target or result or both. This information is included as background information for accountability and discussion with legislators and the general public on public policy issues. However, it is not intended to play a role in budget decision-making.
- *Performance-Informed Budgeting:* In this model, budget resource preparations are indirectly linked to the proposed performance or past achievements by ministries and government agencies. Performance information has an important role but does not have a predetermined weight, nor is it an absolute factor for making decisions on budget allocation. In this sense, performance information is not the only basis but is used along with other information related to political and economic aspects and policy priorities for decision-making on a budget or resource allocation.

- *Direct Performance Budgeting or Performance-Based Budgeting:* In this model, resource allocation is made directly and explicitly based on the unit of performance to be achieved, generally referring to outputs achieved in the year. This form of performance budgeting is used only in specific sectors. For example, the number of students who graduate with a master's degree will determine the following year's funding for the university running the program.

Experiences of OECD member countries have shown that implementing performance-based budgeting is difficult, even in countries with a lot of resources and strong institutions. These budgeting models are used in very few OECD countries. Most are moving towards implementing performance-informed budgeting. Lessons learnt from study visits to Sweden, France, Malaysia and Thailand showed similar challenges and problems, especially at the budget preparation stage.

In Sweden, the Budget Act requires the government to report to the Parliament on performance in terms of implemented policies and measures. At the beginning of each year, the Ministry of Finance places a strong emphasis on gathering performance information, but their efforts did not meet with much success as the line ministries reacted strongly against the use of performance information. This effort caused the generation of too much information and the budget bill already consisted of voluminous documents; it was simply unfeasible for the Ministry of Finance to process all the information and develop a budget. Parliament also voiced concern about the quality of the performance information attached to the budget documents. The use of performance information for budget allocation remained limited.

In France, once the budget has been executed, performance results are included in an Annual Performance Report (APR) attached to the budget. However, the performance results are not used as a basis for the discussion in the Parliament as the information has no direct link to resource allocation. While the reforms provided a high degree of autonomy to program managers in using allocated resources, it was very difficult to make them accountable for results.

Malaysia uses performance indicators extensively in the early stages of resource allocation under what is called Outcome-based Budgeting.

Performance indicators are used in planning to promote better service and program delivery. Greater emphasis is also placed on performance monitoring and evaluation. Program Managers are required to sign agreements in which performance measures are described in detail along with desired goals and then tied to resource allocation. Accountability has enhanced significantly using this process, but transparency has room for improvement among stakeholders in the budget process due to budgetary time constraints.

The Strategic Performance-based Budgeting (SPBB) initiated in Thailand faced several challenges in its implementation. While the SPBB system focuses on outputs and outcomes, in practice, the budgeting process is fundamentally input-based with a limited focus on performance. Budget-to-policy linkages remain input-based, weak and centrally determined. There were also difficulties in determining the right indicators for measuring performance, a lack of technical expertise, information overload, capacity-building issues, and the constant temptation to move back to line-item at both the executive and legislative levels. The resource allocations are not based on performance indicators or conditional on the achievement of performance targets but other economic, political and policy factors are taken into consideration in the decision-making process.

Overall, the utilization of performance information varies from one country to another. Sweden has one of the most developed performance-informed budgeting systems that has evolved over a long time. Similarly, in France, performance information is widely used in the budgeting process, but budget allocation does not entirely depend on performance information. In contrast, Thailand and Malaysia make minimal use of performance information for annual budget preparation and negotiation, but they utilize it widely for reporting purposes.

2.7.4 Performance Informed Budgeting for Cambodia

Cambodia's PFM reform goal is to adopt a performance-based budget. While progress is being made, it is critical for Cambodia to review this ambitious goal to align its efforts with international best practices. As described above, most countries have faced difficulties in implementing performance-based budgeting systems.

Countries that have achieved greater progress in implementing a performance-based budgeting system tend to have a comprehensive results-based management system, where planning, human resource management, and budget management are aligned. They also have a reliable database system that supports better decision-making. Additionally, heads of budget entities are well trained and delegated with sufficient authority to manage budgets and resources.

Cambodia lacks these prerequisites, which prevents the country from implementing a results-based management system in the medium term. In other words, a direct performance-based budgeting system will not be an option for Cambodia soon. A World Bank study that reviewed program budgeting under the framework of the PFMRP recommended that RGC adjust the direction of its budget system reform from performance-based to performance-informed budgeting. The evaluation was done based on experiences gained from piloting a full-fledged budget program over three years. Recent developments in budgeting system reform in other countries also share the same conclusion. As such, Cambodia chose the performance-informed budgeting model to develop its budgeting system, calling its current budget system "Performance Budgeting".

Budget system reform is at the heart of PFMRP and it cannot be isolated from other reforms under PFMRP. The budget system must cut complex processes and provide a simple one to efficiently deliver better public services to citizens, as shown in Figure 3. In other words, with a simpler budget process, it is expected that inefficiency can be reduced and therefore lead to better output and outcome in service delivery. This reform will require coordination with other major reforms, including public administration reform, decentralization and de-concentration reform, national strategic development plan, and audit function reform. The RGC must take a holistic approach to ensure all PFMRP reforms and other major reforms are synchronized and complementary to each other.

Cambodia's budget system reform strategy will mainly focus on the national budget system. It will also need to guide budget system reform to the subnational administration to achieve collective results and national policy objectives by integrating planning, budget management, and reporting systems. This approach should not affect the ongoing decentralization and de-concentration reform. Instead, it should facilitate the transferring of functions and delegate budget execution to subnational administration. Based on an overall assessment of the current status and the complexity of performance budgeting system reforms, the most likely timeframe for achieving this goal is 2025. The budget system reform strategy will therefore cover the reform agenda from 2018 to 2025. The strategy will serve as an orientation principle for public financial management throughout the RGC. All stakeholders will need to ensure their reforms align both in terms of principles and timeframes with the budget reform strategy.

2.8 CROSS-CUTTING REFORM PROGRAMS

The RGC is simultaneously implementing three cross-cutting public sector reforms. Besides the PFM Reform Program, there are two other cross-cutting reform programs. Decentralization and De-concentration Reform (D&D), began in the early 2000s with decision-making and service delivery through the establishment of local democratic institutions meant to increase citizen participation and make government more responsive and accountable. The other cross-cutting program is public administration reform, which is being implemented through the National Program for Administrative Reform under the Ministry of Civil Service.

2.8.1 Decentralization and De-Concentration Reform Program

The legal framework for De-concentration and Decentralization (D&D) reforms is defined by the 2008 Law on Administrative Management of the Capital, Provinces, Municipalities, Districts, and Khans and the 2001 Law on Commune and Sangkat Administration and Management. The two Laws provide for the devolution of functions and assignments to subnational administrations. Two strategic documents that have been developed to guide the implementation of the 2008 Law are the 2005 D&D Strategic Framework and the National Program for Subnational Democratic Development 2010–2019 (2010). While the 2010 National Program provides a reasonable strategic framework, some aspects of the law are not clearly articulated yet and the roles, functions and authorities of different tiers of government require further clarity.

The D&D reforms are led by the Ministry of Interior (MOI) with the main implementation and coordination role assigned to the National Committee for Democratic Development (NCDD). The nature of this reform is very complex as it involves many provinces, ministries and institutions. At the same time, D&D reform also involves public administrative reform and the PFM Reform Program.

Subnational administrative reform has been moving forward but is constrained by the lack of staff and institutional capacity. However, decentralization is always a slow and calibrated process. In moving forward, underlying governance arrangements and institutional capacities for reform will need to be further strengthened.

In terms of financing arrangements for Subnational Administrations (SNAs), in principle, all SNAs receive subsidies or transfers of resources to cover expenditure gaps from the national level. Currently, there are a total of 185 Municipalities and Districts and 1,646 *Sangkats* and Communes that are funded almost entirely by transfers from the government. A substantial portion of the total provincial funding is sourced from tax and non-tax revenues, while the rest comes through government transfers, driven by necessities and the availability of funds.

Like any decentralization reform, there are inherent risks in transferring the functions. Public service delivery will deteriorate without corresponding funds and the lack of capacity and this, in turn, will affect the overall quality of the administration. International experiences show that there are risks in the processes of transferring functions to SNAs. As stated earlier, there are similarities between the subnational administration structure in Cambodia and that of France. The experiences of D&D in France are based primarily on the nature of the functions to be delegated and the capacity of the regional authorities to undertake them effectively and efficiently. Hence, the capacity of SNAs and the efficiency and effectiveness in the delivery of programs are the key criteria for determining which functions will be transferred. Programs of strategic nature revolving around national strategies will be nationally managed. For example, the national strategic programs involving health and education are driven and implemented nationally. Supporting programs such as managing facilities and buildings may be decentralized to the regional authorities but with specific guidelines.

The RGC developed a risk management mechanism for determining the delegation of authority to the SNAs. Nevertheless, the effective implementation of the delegation remains a challenge. To support the subnational budget system reform, Cambodia is suggested to consider certain long-term measures as priorities, such as assuring institutional readiness, increasing staff capacity and skills, tightening financial compliance and developing a clear framework for accountability.

2.8.2 Public Administration Reform Program

The improvements in public sector performance have been incremental and slow largely as a result of the wholesale destruction of the civil service and institutions during the civil strife in the 1970s and 1980s. While there have been marked improvements, human resources in the public sector are still not sufficiently developed to ensure the efficient delivery of public services. In recognizing the constraints and the need for a modern and efficient public service, the RGC has committed to reform public administration, establishing the Ministry of Civil Service (MCS) to develop and strengthen the civil service. The MCS and the Committee for Public Administrative Reform developed the National Program for Administrative Reform (NPAR). The NPAR has three main objectives: (1) promote high quality, reliable, and responsive public service; (2) improve civil servants' performance, with strict adherence to the culture of service, ownership, and professionalism; and (3) reform the pay system to ensure equity, improve productivity and work effectiveness.

The implementation of the NPAR has made remarkable progress towards its objectives, but there are some challenges that require systematic and comprehensive attention. These include the oversight of operations, institutions and entities at both national and subnational levels, rationalization of the size of public service, and the organizational structure of ministries, institutions, and subnational administrations. The civil service is also constrained by the lack of integration of reforms into action plans of governmental units both at national and subnational levels.

To address these challenges, and in line with the RGC's focus on the result-based approach to public sector reforms, the MCS has introduced a

National Program for Public Administration Reform 2020–30 with a vision to ensure a citizen-based public administration that is strong, transparent, and capable. To achieve this vision, this national program set three stages: The first stage expected for implementation in 2020–23 focuses on strengthening performance in public administration, the second stage (2023–27) will focus on implementing and evaluating performance-based management systems in public administration, and the third one (2027–30) will focus on performance accountability in public services.

2.8.3 Cross-Cutting Issues of the Reforms

The three cross-cutting reform initiatives are interconnected. D&D, which involves a major rebalancing of the state apparatus, provides the backdrop to the other two reforms, which are more focused on reforming specific functions of the government: human resource management in public administration reform, and government finance in PFM. When combined, the three reforms have the potential to substantially improve public sector performance and service delivery for Cambodian citizens.

Human resource capacity development is a prerequisite for the successful implementation of D&D and PFM reforms. Putting a greater emphasis on performance in budget decisions requires considerable coordination between all levels of government, which in turn calls for greater access to consistent information.

Civil servants are now compensated with a living wage. However, this has not yet been accompanied by adequate incentives to ensure that a core set of behaviours are followed by civil servants. More broadly, any changes arising from a review of the civil service will likely impact the operations of key ministries and SNAs. If managed well, the public administration reform process can potentially address barriers to decentralization, eventually enabling the flow of funds to SNAs. Resistance from powerful interests to these reforms should be expected, making careful implementation of the change management processes necessary.

Each of the three reform programs has its leadership, vision and organizational framework. Nevertheless, many cross-cutting issues have to be solved through all three reform programs. As a result, the chairman of each reform committee has created a coordination mechanism through their secretariats. Each reform secretariat takes turns to chair quarterly meetings where cross-cutting challenges are discussed and solutions are proposed.

Yet despite this coordination, challenges remain. Even though a joint work plan for the three reform secretariats began in 2016, it consists of independent activities and does not cover a common vision for the three reforms. It sometimes appears that the three reform initiatives do not share a common goal and lack higher-level guidance. To address this issue, the PFMSC decided on the Vision and Strategy for 3+1 Reform Program, of which the law and justice reform was included.

2.9 SUMMARY

This chapter provides a brief overview of the historical development of the Cambodian economy and introduces the PFM reform program. Before the start of the PFM reform program, the RGC faced serious fiscal deficits and relied largely on external grants and loans to close financial gaps. In December 2004, Public Financial Management Reform Program was launched as one of the key reform agendas of the government. It was conducted in stages. Stage 1 (2005–8) focused on achieving budget credibility through increasing revenue mobilization and improving the predictability of the overall budget execution. Stage 2 (2009–15) focused on financial accountability in government agencies. Stage 3 (2016–20) focused on the linkage between each ministry's budget allocation and policies. Despite many achievements in Platform 3, the RGC had decided to extend CAP3 for two years more. This decision aimed to further strengthen the foundation of achievement in Platform 3 before stepping into Platform 4, which is expected to be implemented between 2023 and 2027.

In terms of institutional arrangement, the General Secretariat of the Public Financial Management Reform Steering Committee (GSC) is responsible for: (1) designing policies, strategies, and consolidated action plans; (2) preparing quarterly and annual reports on issues facing PFM with proposed solutions; (3) coordinating with general departments within MEF to action plans; (4) monitoring and evaluating the implementation of PFM. In the aspect of budget system, Cambodia adopted the performance-informed budgeting system which fits the Cambodian context.

The PFM reform program in Cambodia has been conducted with technical and financial support from development partners and the strong leadership of the government.

NOTES
1. Cambodia Public Expenditure Review, World Bank, 1999.
2. *Cambodian Public Debt Statistic Bulletin* Vol. 9, Data as of Year-end 2019, issued in March 2020.
3. The platform approach is a strategic approach to reform, that attempts to maximize reform impact by programming reform actions in a sequenced way to support further reforms and is cast in a multi-year framework. (*Guidelines for Sequencing PFM Reform*, Jack Diamond, July 2012.)
4. Currently, DPs are led by European Union, with the Asia Development Bank as the co-chair.
5. Report of mid-term budget execution evaluation and estimation of implementing 2020 budget law.
6. *Cambodian Public Debt Statistic Bulletin* Vol. 9, Data as of Year-end 2019, issued in March 2020.
7. The report of the PFM and TWG meeting on the 2019 progress report of the PFM reform program stage 3.
8. *Cambodian Garment and Footwear Sector Bulletin*, Issue 7, June 2018.
9. The practice of rethinking and redesigning the way work is done to better support an organization's mission and reduce costs.
10. To address this issue, the MEF introduced the strategic plan for streamlining the business process 2020–25 and the change management plan.
11. To address this issue, the MEF introduced the law on State Property Management and Utilization and State Asset Register Management Information System-SARMIS in 2020.

CHAPTER THREE

Strategic Planning and Budgeting

The potential benefits of effective medium-term budgeting have been extensively documented. A well-designed and well-managed framework for medium-term budgeting contributes to better fiscal discipline and control, increased efficiency in resource allocation, and improved cost-effectiveness of service delivery by enhancing clarity in policy objectives, predictability in budget allocation, and accountability and transparency in the use of resources. For Cambodia, it starts with preparing the fiscal framework, now called the Medium-Term Macroeconomic and Public Finance Framework (MMPFF) that is aligned with global macroeconomic outlooks, RGC's policy priorities, and revenue and expenditure trends.

The Budget System Reform Strategy (BSRS) describes three elements for forming the budget planning framework:

1. Medium-Term Macroeconomic and Public Finance Framework;
2. Medium-Term Budget Framework (MTBF); and
3. Budget Strategic Plans at ministries, institutions and provincial levels.

The MMPFF is currently used for the preparation of the budget law but is to be phased out and replaced by the Medium-Term Fiscal Framework (MTFF) between 2025 and 2027,[1] starting at the commencement of the 2023 budget law preparation. The introduction of the MTFF and MTBF will strengthen medium-term budgeting in the annual budget process. These two tools will be critical for developing economic policy in Cambodia. The budget process operates on a three-year rolling basis, covering the budget for the immediate year and two years after, to ensure a truly medium-term outlook for budget planning.

3.1 MEDIUM-TERM FISCAL FRAMEWORK

The MTFF is a macroeconomic model that provides the basis to forecast growth by economic sector, inflation, interest rates, exchange rates and potential revenues and expenditures. These forecasts are based on assumptions of the sectoral interaction in the economy as well as the potential impact of shocks in the world economy. The reliability of the forecast is dependent upon the accuracy of the economic model and its assumptions, which attempt to reflect the actual status of the economy.

The MTFF will be part of a transparent planning and budget formulation process that will attempt to link government policies and priorities to resource allocation. It is designed to ensure overall fiscal discipline by setting fiscal targets and allocating the resultant resources to strategic priorities within these targets. The Rectangular Strategy (RS) and National Strategy Development Plan (NSDP) are the primary strategic policy inputs to the MTFF.

The MTFF sets out a fiscal strategy and fiscal policy stance by determining the total revenue and expenditure for the medium term. It will describe expenditure ceilings for four broad governmental sectors: General Administration, National Defense and Public Order, the Social Sector, and the Economic Sector. MTFF will bind the total spending ceiling of the first year and provide indicative ceilings for the subsequent two years based on available resources, macroeconomic conditions, and fiscal targets.

The MTFF will guide budget planning and significant input into the MTBF, setting the foundation for realistic and focused discussions on budget allocations between the General Department of Budget (GDB) and spending entities. It will also help the spending entities prepare realistic expenditure plans.

While the MTFF is currently premised on the maintenance of the strong macroeconomic performance of recent years, the macroeconomic outlook remains vulnerable worldwide, due to the COVID-19 epidemic, meaning significant fiscal risks will need to be carefully managed.

3.2 MEDIUM-TERM BUDGET FRAMEWORK
What Is Medium-Term Budget Framework?
Fiscal budgeting focuses on preparing an annual plan for revenue and

expenditure. However, a multi-year budget process allows for early announcements of policy changes that will be implemented later. These warnings of a future change in a ministry's budget help to manage expectations and allow budget managers to prepare for forthcoming increases or cuts in resources. Advanced warnings can alleviate some of the resistance typically met when a budget reduction is proposed. The budget negotiations' added time dimensions also help the government deal with proposals for new spending. Within a strictly annual budget horizon, a particular proposal can be met only with a binary yes or no. A medium-term horizon provides the option of committing to introducing the proposal in a future budget if sufficient fiscal space is available.

Cambodia's MTBF document is developed along with the MMPFF, which is soon to become the MTFF. It is under the direction of the Budget System Reform Strategy, a key piece of the PFM Reform Project. Having the fiscal framework strengthens fiscal planning and improves macro-fiscal projections, which in turn provides a stronger basis for the MTBF.

Guided by the estimates provided in the fiscal framework, the MTBF focuses on institutional arrangements for prioritizing and presenting LM- and agency-level policy priorities and expenditure ceilings. The MTBF essentially provides the link between the fiscal framework and the BSP by integrating policy, planning, and budgeting within the medium-term perspective.

The Budget Strategic Plan (BSP) sets the high-level parameters for each newly created annual budget. The quality and comprehensiveness of the BSP are critical in ensuring that national policy priorities are cascaded down to the implementation levels and have sufficient rigour to measure their performance and report the results of aggregate performance up to the national level. MTBF provides the link between national policy aggregates and strategic plans at the LMs and agencies.

Program managers have to be trained in strategic planning and program logic models to establish linkages between budget and policy priorities. This includes the identification of performance areas and developing the right indicator for measuring performance. The focus on capacity building represents a significant change management goal for PFM reform and must be done holistically to cover the entire budgeting process, including the fiscal framework of the MTBF and the BSP.

The move to program budgeting in Cambodia required a holistic view of all government activities in order to reduce redundant activities and better manage limited resources. Most activities across the government will be integrated into the MTBF, which has been improved to capture all resources required for the activities. Wages and capital expenditure components are included in the budget proposal for all ministries and agencies. In addition, Public Investment Management (PIM) will also be included in the budget process, creating a three-year rolling public investment program to be streamlined and integrated into the medium-term budget preparation process.

Because achieving national policy objectives involves the activities of several ministries and agencies, the contributions of each program have to be identified, coordinated, planned, and resourced. In addition, performance needs to be monitored for each activity and by each ministry and agency. MEF has set up a system to manage this process through the MTBF. Timely budget and expenditure data are vital in deciding expenditure ceilings and this information must also be complemented with credible performance information. While the BSP provides the necessary strategic framework, the MTBF captures relevant performance information and establishes program linkages.

For the budget year 2020, the MTBF was prepared by the General Department of Budget of MEF and submitted to the Prime Minister for advice and direction. The MTBF was then sent to the Council of Ministers for adoption and subsequently submitted to the Prime Minister for endorsement.

There is no single method of setting expenditure ceilings. Ceilings were introduced to control spending. Ceilings can be decided based on meeting specific objectives, budget performances and capacity constraints. However, once a criterion has been set, it has to be applied across all levels of government. The establishment of ceilings within the medium term is the result of a complex set of negotiations between national and sector policy priorities and their implementation through ministries and agencies. Generally, expense ceilings are widely credited through strengthening fiscal discipline, improving the strategic allocation of public resources, and establishing a baseline for future improvements. At the ministries and agencies, expenditure ceilings and floor signify a realistic resource envelope for planning. They allow ministries and agencies to plan realistically and look for savings and efficiency.

3.3 BUDGET STRATEGIC PLAN

The Budget Strategic Plan (BSP) is a three-year rolling plan that ministries and agencies need to prepare annually through a top-down approach by linking their policy priorities to sectoral goals and the National Strategic Development Plan. The BSP is prepared by policy and program objectives and includes program descriptions and rationales, sources of financing, key performance targets, timeframes and budget requirements.

When preparing the BSP, it is also necessary to consider program funding requirements that come on a recurrent basis (e.g., wage expenses, operational expenses, maintenance, utilities, etc.). These expenditures are not directly related to outcomes but are still necessary. For such programs, the emphasis is on inputs, outputs and operational efficiency improvement, rather than policy performance and program effectiveness.

BSPs also need to be comprehensive through progressive expansion by including coverage of all sources of financing, such as state budgets, development partners funds/budgets and own sources of revenues,[2] and all types of expenditures, including current expenses, capital expenses, grant financing, subsidies, and resource transfers. In this regard, the BSP is a crucial tool for integrating current and capital budgets.

The medium-term investment plan for financing through loans is prepared separately for each development partner. These externally funded investments are integrated into the list of the three-year rolling Public Investment Program (PIP) prepared by the Ministry of Planning, together with the public investment projects financed under grants from development partners through the Council for the Development of Cambodia (CDC). MEF is responsible for preparing the annual budget for capital expenditures financed by external partners based on a three-year rolling list of public investment programmes. For the domestically financed capital budget, there is no medium-term plan yet. The challenges of fully integrating both types of financing are:

- The medium-term budget plans and public investment plans have two different time frames as large investment projects will be subject to

special approvals, based on their long-term financial obligations, which are beyond the standard timeframe of budget planning;
- The two different planning processes (public investment programming and recurrent budget formulation) are carried out by two different agencies and at different timelines.

One objective of BSP is to improve the financial integration of both current and capital budgets during annual budget formulation. Project proposals are prepared by the ministries and agencies as part of BSP preparation with justifications for achieving respective program objectives. In this regard, it is necessary to develop a clear Public Investment Management framework (PIM) as the basis for the preparation and approval of the medium-term investment budget.

3.4 ANNUAL BUDGETING

Budget Formulation

Currently, once approval of the fiscal framework, the GDB will issue an instructive circular calling for the preparation of the BSPs. This triggers the first stage of the budget formulation process when ministries and agencies prepare their BSPs include elements of cost increases and new proposals for the budget year within the budget ceilings provided. This stage takes place from March to May.

The preparation of the budget is the second phase, taking place from June to September. After guidelines on how to prepare the budget are adopted by the Council of Ministers in June, individual government units provide details on their revenue and expenditure and send them to MEF. This begins the process of budget discussions. The final stage, from October to December, is the budget approval stage, where a draft law is sent to the Council of Ministers for approval, then to the National Assembly, and finally to Senate during the first week of December. The calendar for budget preparation is very clear and if the law cannot be passed, the previous year's management and budget are used. Figures 3.1 and 3.2 demonstrate the budget preparation cycle and the budget structure.

Annual Budget Cycle

The annual budget is currently prepared on an incremental basis to support the continuation of public service for another year. The budget is adjusted

FIGURE 3.1
Budget Preparation Cycle

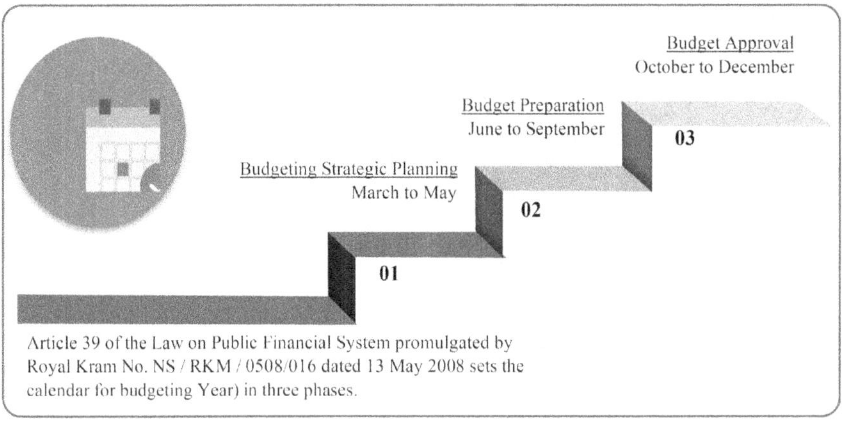

- **01** Budgeting Strategic Planning — March to May
- **02** Budget Preparation — June to September
- **03** Budget Approval — October to December

Article 39 of the Law on Public Financial System promulgated by Royal Kram No. NS / RKM / 0508/016 dated 13 May 2008 sets the calendar for budgeting Year) in three phases.

Source: Authors' illustration.

based on wage increases, the net increase of personnel, the previous year's budget implementation, and unexpected price changes. Each ministry and institution can request an additional budget consistent with their three-year medium-term Budget Strategic Plan (BSP) and within the incremental rate set forth as the ceiling for ministries, which defend their proposals with MEF at budget discussion meetings. See Figure 3.3.

The annual budget reflects both the linkages between sector policies and MMPFF (later changed to MTFF) and between MTBF and the BSP as shown in Figure 3.4. Sector policies and MMPFF are developed based on the national policies (Rectangular Strategy and National Strategic Development Plan). Figure 3.5 illustrates the relationship between the policy structure (policy objectives, programs and activities) and organizational management structure (leadership, management, and technical level) with clear roles and responsibilities in a transparent and accountable manner.

The objective for 2025 is that the discussion on the budget proposal, both current and capital budgets, will principally be based on program performance, which will help achieve program objectives, outputs, and outcomes, and improve efficiency. The discussion on the proposed budget will remain on an annual incremental basis but with increased flexibility. LMs must make every effort to reduce expenditures relative to the previous-

FIGURE 3.2
Budget Structure

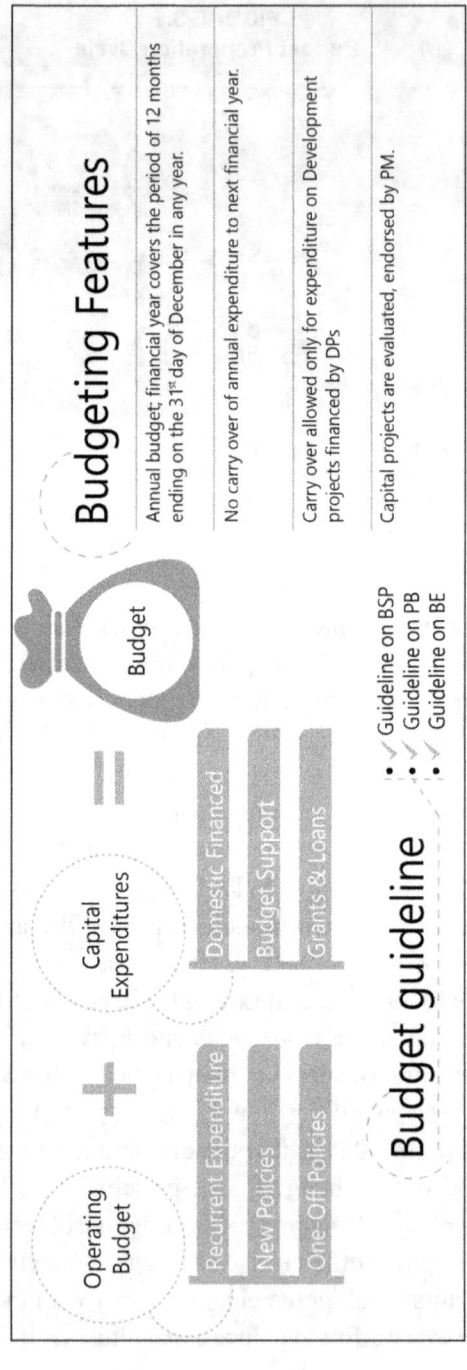

Source: Authors' Illustration.

50 • *Public Financial Management: Cambodian Experiences*

**FIGURE 3.3
Annual Budget Cycle**

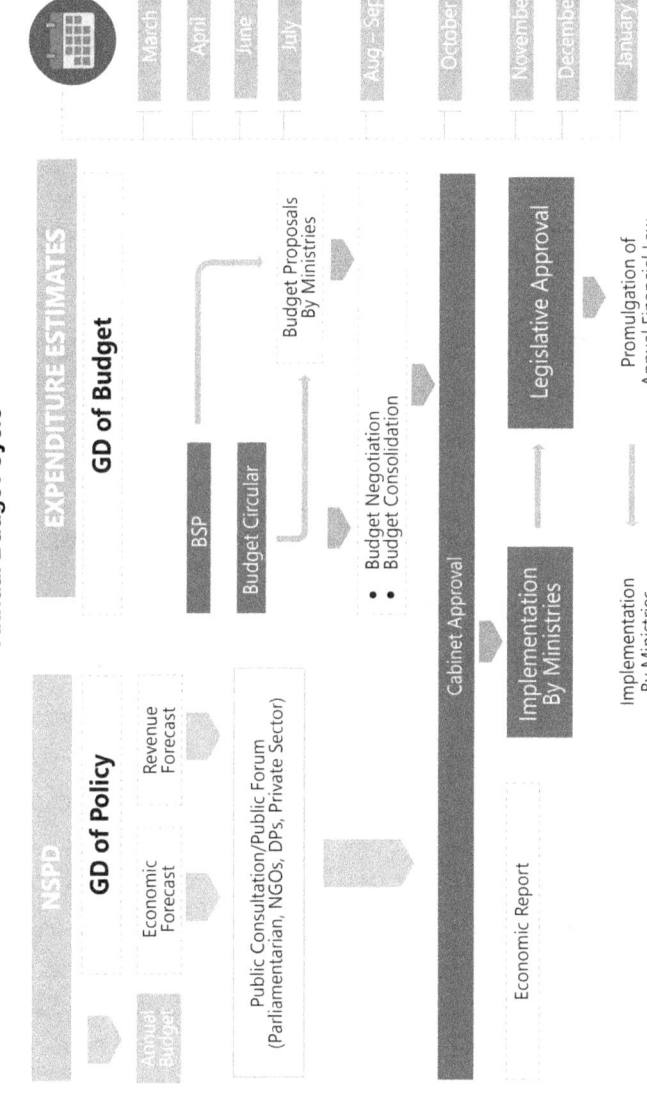

Source: Authors' illustration.

FIGURE 3.4
Linkage of National Priorities and Sector Policies

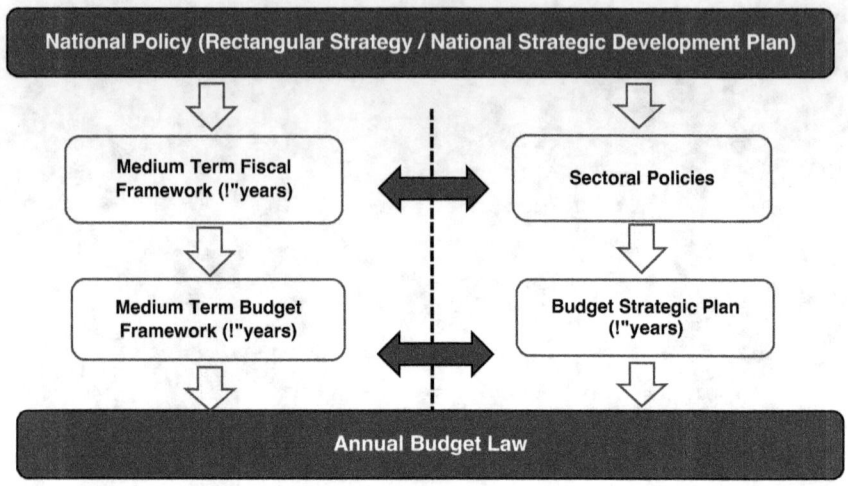

Source: Cambodia Budget System Reform Strategy 2018–2025 (2018).

FIGURE 3.5
Linkage-Organizational Structure, Role and Responsibility and Program Structure

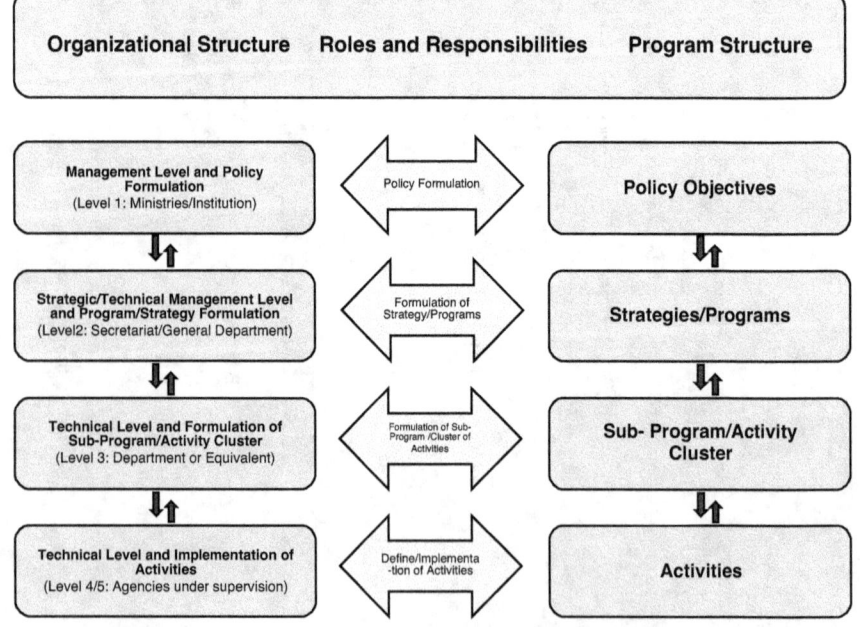

Source: Cambodia Budget System Reform Strategy 2018–2025 (2018).

year budget so that funds can be reallocated and resources are redeployed as much as possible.

Budget preparation will fully utilize all seven budget classifications within the Financial Management Information System (FMIS). These budget classifications are economic, administrative, functional, geographical, program, source of funds and project. The economic classification will only apply to certain types of expenditure, allowing for greater flexibility in the use of funds for implementing programs, subprograms and clusters of activities.

Budget Review and Approval

The process of approving an annual budget is sequenced following the calendar for drafting the annual budget law. Generally, this principle has been adhered to, and each ministry and agency will have a period of six weeks to prepare their respective budgets. After the government's endorsement, the draft Annual Budget Law is submitted to the legislature for review and approval.

Currently, the review of the draft Annual Budget Law in the Legislature is done by the Economic, Finance, Banking, and Auditing Committee, the so-called "Second Committee", with the participation of other relevant committees. The MEF is responsible, on behalf of LMs, for defending the draft Annual Budget Law, both in the Second Committee and at the Plenary Session of the Legislature, following the Law on Public Finance System 2008.

By 2025, the Annual Budget Law will be revised and enhanced. Budget debates at the program level will be held at the relevant specialized committees of the two legislative bodies organized by the National Assembly; relevant specialized committees of the Senate will be able to participate in these debates. The LMs will be responsible for defending their programs and budgets at these specialized Committee meetings. The annual budget discussion at the Plenary Session of the Legislative Bodies will focus on policy objectives at the ministry/agency level and the overall budget envelope.

Over time, the National Assembly will approve, chapter by chapter, the draft law that will include policy objectives, program classification and a simplified economic classification. By 2025, the draft Annual Budget Law will include performance information as an annexe, which will play an important role in providing program information for evaluation purposes.

The New Budget System

After two years of piloting comprehensive program budgeting reform, the review by both the PFMR Steering Committee and the World Bank concluded that "Cambodia has made good progress in implementing program budgeting." The review found that one key to the progress was the introduction of the Budget Strategic Plan. The setting of policy goals, programs, and indicators in the BSP was recognized as a positive feature for further promoting the focus on performance. Improving the conditions of budget estimation also provided a good environment for budget planning.

In fact, budget reform goes back many years. After completing the piloting stage of partial program budgeting in 2014, the full-fledge piloting of program budgeting was introduced to ten LMs in 2015 and expanded to thirty-six LMs and agencies in 2017, along with implementation in six provincial administrations. Following this direction, all ministries and agencies were required to implement full program budgeting by 2018. They were required to prepare their annual budget by policy objectives, programs, subprograms and activities for budget negotiation, and these programs were to be directly implemented by the budget entities of LMs and agencies of the RGC. However, during this piloting period, the budget will continue to be prepared on a line-item basis and remains the official budget document to be submitted to the legislature for review and approval.

The roll-out of the program budget reform is working well, with annual budget preparation becoming more comprehensive and realistic. As shown in Figure 3.6, the determination of policy objectives, programs, and subprograms in the BSP has made the preparation and implementation of program budgeting more efficient and manageable. In addition, MEF provided a substantial amount of training, technical support and guidance to LMs and agencies, which improved the implementation of program budgeting, and in turn, the implementation of program budgeting gained

**FIGURE 3.6
Program Budgeting Structure**

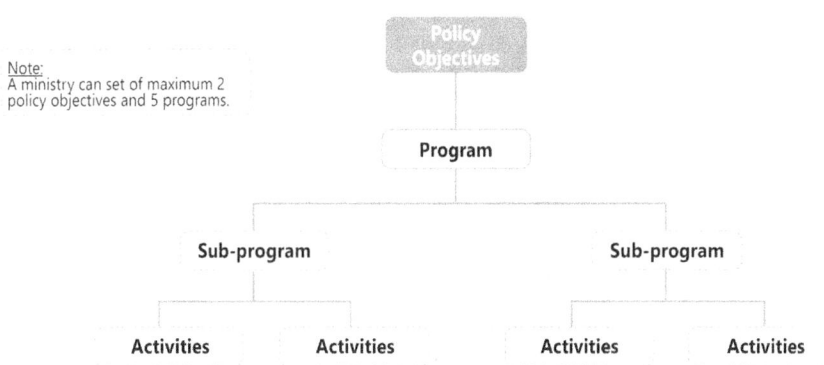

Source: Authors' illustration.

active support and participation from LMs and agencies, at both the political and technical levels. The example of Program Budget for the Ministry of Education, Youth and Sports shows significant improvement in program and subprogram structure and expected outcomes (Figure 3.7)

3.5 SUMMARY

This chapter discusses the strategic planning and budgeting process of the government. So far, the MMPFF has been used as a tool to predict the overall macroeconomic situation and to help prepare the budget. However, this framework will be replaced by the MTFF and MTBF to provide more leeway in budget preparation, using a three-year rolling period rather than on a single-year basis.

The new MTTF is considered a necessary tool to promote policy and priority responsiveness by providing the foundation for realistic and focused discussions on budget allocations between the General Department of Budget (GDB) and spending entities. The MTTF will set the parameters of the government's fiscal strategy and fiscal policy by determining its total revenue and expenditure over the medium term. In principle, MTFF adheres to two fiscal anchors, namely: (1) the debt-to-GDP ratio; and (2) the maintenance of government deposits with the banking system at comfortable levels.

FIGURE 3.7
Example: Program Budget for Ministry of Education, Youth and Sports

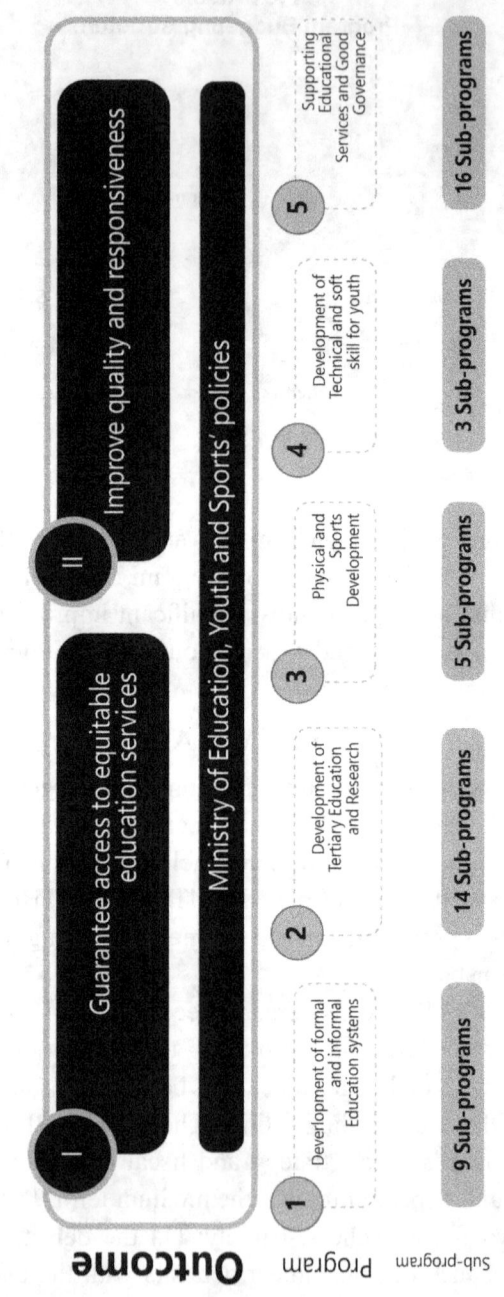

Source: Authors' illustration.

Based on the amounts of total revenue and expenditure determined by the MTFF, MTBF will focus on the institutional arrangement for prioritizing expenditures with LMs and agencies. However, it is critically important that program managers in LMs are properly trained in strategic planning so that they can establish the link between budget and policy priorities. The measurability of performance is also essential for providing feedback for future improvements.

The BSP is a three-year rolling plan, taking into consideration all sources of government financing—including state budgets, development partner budgets and own sources of revenues—and all types of expenditure, such as current expenses, capital expenses, grant financing, subsidies, and resource transfers.

NOTES

1. The MTFF was to be started for implementation in 2021–23, but it was delayed to 2023–25 due to the economic uncertainty resulting from the COVID-19 pandemic. It was later decided that the MTFF will be put into use between 2025 and 2027.
2. Own source revenue is defined as revenue raised by a government from its own imposition of a tax, a licence, a fee or any other charge.

CHAPTER FOUR

Components of PFM in Cambodia

The components of public financial management in Cambodia are: (1) revenue management, (2) public expenditure management, (3) public investment management, (4) public debt management, (5) state property management, (6) public procurement management, (7) public accounting system, (8) FMIS, and (9) control system. This chapter will explain how the PFMRP efforts modernize each component.

4.1 REVENUE MANAGEMENT

Government revenue refers to the money received by a government from both taxes and non-tax sources. Government revenues and expenditures are the two primary components of the government budget and essential tools of the government's fiscal policy. Without sufficient revenues and proper management of them, the government would not be able to provide adequate public services to its citizens, from fire brigades and police to environmental protection and telecommunications.

Cambodia has achieved significant revenue growth in recent years. However, the recent global COVID-19 pandemic is providing a monumental challenge to the country's ability to sustain the government's recent levels of revenue, particularly in key sectors such as tourism and garment manufacturing exports.

4.1.1 Key Objective in Domestic Revenue Mobilization

Strengthening domestic revenue mobilization (meaning revenue generated within the Cambodian economy) has played a key role in transforming

Cambodia from a low-income to a lower-middle-income country in 2015. Its role will be even more critical as the RGC works towards achieving an upper-middle income by 2030 and high-income status by 2050. As the country's income per capita increases, Cambodia's external financing is expected to be reduced in the medium to long term. This requires Cambodia to work harder to mobilize both short- and medium-term revenue to achieve high economic growth and maintain a robust economic system that is sustainable, resilient to crisis, and responsive to development needs.

The government launched a highly successful Medium-Term Revenue Mobilization Strategy 2014–18, which substantially increased domestic revenue. Through this effort, the share of current revenue to GDP increased significantly from 10.3 per cent in 2004 to 15.0 per cent in 2013 and continued to grow to 22.0 per cent in 2018. This growth rate is even more remarkable in recent years, with an average growth of approximately 1.4 per cent per year from 2013 to 2018 (Figure 4.1).

The main reasons for this achievement can be attributed to three factors:

(1) the enhancement of the tax culture: the rate of timely tax payment has increased due to enhanced payment conveniences, improvement in

FIGURE 4.1
Current Revenue Achievements, 2013–18

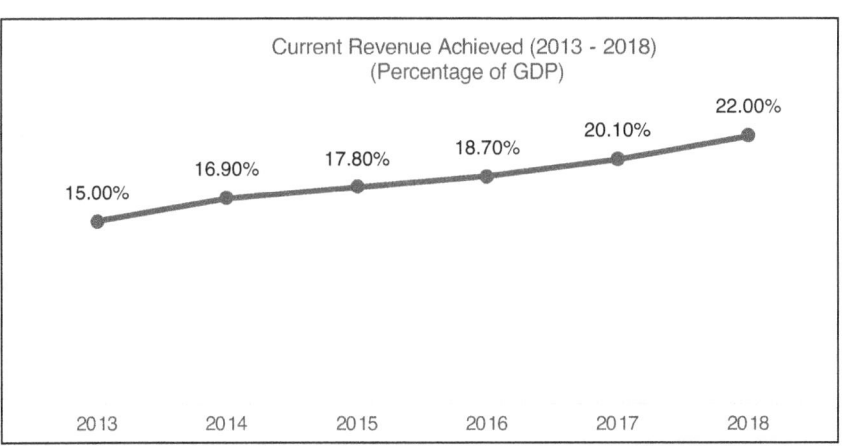

Source: Ministry of Economy and Finance, "Report on Monitoring and Evaluation of Implementing Revenue Mobilization Strategy 2014–2018" (2019).

the quality of taxpayer services, as well as the review of some fiscal policies that facilitated trade and contributed to strengthening the tax payment to the state;
(2) modernization of tax administration by implementing reform measures for both tax and non-tax administration; and
(3) optimization of the efficiency of mobilizing revenue. Ideally, tax collection should be in line with its projections for better budget planning. The unexpected increase in tax revenues is a good thing, but there is room for more accurate forecasting.

With this achievement in the implementation of the Revenue Mobilization Strategy Phase I, the government continues to develop and implement a new revenue mobilization strategy for 2019–23 aiming to sustain economic growth, maintain sustainable incomes, ensure the fairness of revenue collection to taxpayers and improve the efficiency of revenue collection and management. The objective is to meet government expenditure requirements for the sustainability of state operations and development.

The 2019–23 strategy addresses key challenges to mobilizing revenue. First, certain past fiscal policies mainly focused on increasing revenue but did not fully address socio-economic and environmental impacts, especially concerning attracting investment, promoting competitiveness, and diversifying the economy. In many ways, some of the formulation of fiscal policies in the past have also not been consistent with national development policy. In addition, the administration of both tax and non-tax revenue has not responded as envisaged due to the increased workload on civil servants. Finally, the equity and fairness of revenue collection were less than hoped for. Implementing the second phase of the revenue mobilization strategy will move the government towards modernizing the state revenue system and better meeting its development needs. In this regard, the revenue mobilization strategy for 2019–23 will be an important policy tool to mobilize state revenue effectively and efficiently.

4.1.2 Types of Revenue

There are two types of government revenues—current revenue and capital revenue. Current revenue refers to the money received by the government on a regular or day-to-day basis. The vast majority of this revenue comes from taxation, but additional revenue is generated through customs and excise charges. On the other hand, capital revenue refers to irregular or once-off revenue generated by the government from such sources as capital projects (loans and grants), and income generated by the government, such as government-owned corporation incomes and central bank revenue.

4.1.3 Current Revenue

The amount of current revenue is what the government expects to collect each year, making it a *recurrent* source of revenue. Recurrent revenue is planned for both tax and non-tax revenue. The MEF is directly responsible for determining the amount of the tax and non-tax revenue that is subject to collecting and estimating the tax and non-tax revenue collected from public enterprises. All line ministries and agencies as well as governors of the capital and provinces send estimates for expected revenue to the MEF for the revenue planning section of the budget. The Government has strengthened the tax and non-tax administrations by promoting a new culture of taxation and compliance, differentiating from the past practices of rampant tax avoidance. The number of tax audits has substantially increased, and there is an ongoing enhancement of efficiency and effectiveness in revenue collection to meet the growing market economy needs with encouraging results. Although the tax and non-tax administrations have achieved good performance and progress, some major challenges still exist and require all administrations to pay further attention and consider implementing measures to modernize both tax administration and policy.

4.1.4 Tax Revenue

Tax revenue includes income from domestic taxes, taxes on foreign trade, and other tax revenues. The tax revenue amounts are determined by the law and collected and monitored by the MEF. Tax rates, tax bases, tax exemptions, and the settlement of disputes related to the collection and control of taxes are determined within the framework prescribed in the laws relating to each tax category. Domestic revenue, which is the main driver of recurrent revenue, increased from 8.5 per cent of GDP in 2004 to 12.7 per cent of GDP in 2013 and grew to approximately 19.2 per cent of GDP in 2018. Domestic tax revenue includes an input value-added tax (VAT) (KHR2,619 billion), an import special tax (KHR3,304 billion), customs duties (KHR1,594 billion), income tax (KHR3,192 billion), and an output VAT (KHR2,101 billion).

This achievement reflects the efforts of both the General Department of Customs and Excise and the General Department of Taxation which collect tax revenue. These departments have continued to reform and modernize tax administration by improving fiscal policy based on the principles of simplification, transparency, equity, fairness, and efficiency. Building and strengthening the capacity of tax administration has played an important role in fostering positive changes in economic structure, technology, business environment, and taxpayer behaviour.

4.1.5 Customs and Excise Revenue

The General Department of Customs and Excise (GDCE) is responsible for the management, control and collection of taxes and fees on exported or imported goods in accordance with customs and other laws and regulations, including the prevention of smuggling. GDCE also participates in international trade policy discussions and promotes international practices relating to customs controls and trade facilitation.

Since 1999, GDCE has been implementing five consecutive strategies for customs reform and modernization to strengthen customs administration in terms of structure, professionalism and operational procedures aimed at mobilizing revenue to the fullest extent possible. Through the implementation of the Customs Reform and Modernization Program, as shown in Figure 4.2, the GDCE has achieved a substantial increase in revenue collection.

The factors that contributed to this increase can be attributed to the following:

- regular updating of the customs data valuation system,
- strengthening the prevention of tax evasion,
- assessing trader risk indicators and regularly updating them,
- determining minimum data required on commercial invoices,
- strengthening customs technical work and privacy compliance, and

FIGURE 4.2
Custom and Excise Revenue, 2013–18

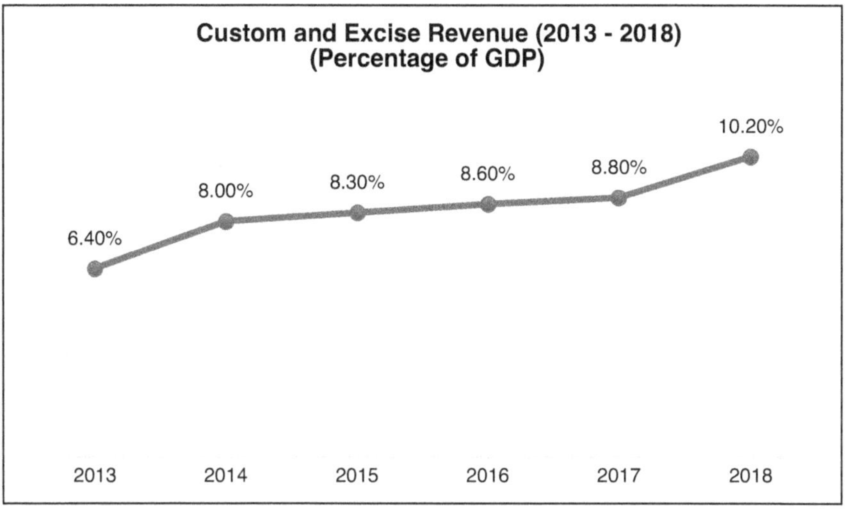

Custom and Excise Revenue (2013 - 2018)
(Percentage of GDP)

2013	2014	2015	2016	2017	2018
6.40%	8.00%	8.30%	8.60%	8.80%	10.20%

Source: Ministry of Economy and Finance, "Report on Monitoring and Evaluation of Implementing Revenue Mobilization Strategy 2014–2018" (2019).

- facilitating trade through automation and simplification of customs procedures.

GDCE has reformed business processes and operations by modernizing the IT system, operationalizing one-window service, revising guidelines and processes of container scanning, accepting certificates of origin from recognized exporters, and addressing challenges and requests of the private sector.

There are also several challenges yet to be fully addressed, including the limited culture for tax payments that keeps smuggling and tax evasion popular. The wider implementation of free trade agreements is also a factor affecting customs revenue, as a result of the government's commitment to tariff reduction and/or elimination. In addition, the revenue from the import of automobiles and petroleum makes up more than 60 per cent of total customs revenue during 2014–18, an indication of the narrow base of customs revenue.

The implementation of the 2019–23 revenue mobilization strategy will play an important role in addressing some of the remaining issues as the strategy will focus on:

(1) Facilitating trade to reduce costs and time taken by traders to fulfil customs duties for international trade.
(2) Improving and strengthening governance to promote compliance and assure revenue sustainability by strengthening auditing and monitoring of business locations, which will further enhance the effectiveness of preventing and suppressing customs offences.
(3) Strengthening the management of customs revenue sources and developing human resources in a quantity and quality that will meet modernization needs and help in promoting revenue sustainability.

4.1.6 Tax Reform Efforts

The General Department of Taxation (GDT) carries out the policies established by MEF regarding tax laws and regulations. The department collects tax revenue for the RGC's coffers, provides taxpayers with educational information and guidance, conducts audits, implements punitive measures, and enforces penalties in accordance with tax laws and regulations. It seeks to optimize management through clear policies, processes, and working systems that are modern and highly responsive.

In line with PFM reform, GDT developed its own five-year rolling operational strategic plan to increase revenue collection. GDT's tax revenue ratio to GDP was up from 1.9 per cent in 2002 to 5.8 per cent in 2013 and 9.0 per cent in 2018 (Figure 4.3).

GDT's contribution to the total tax revenue rose from 27 per cent in 2002 to 46 per cent in 2013. This result was achieved by the high growth of receipts in major tax categories such as local VAT, tax on income, tax on salaries and tax revenue from the subnational sector. In addition, GDT has also:

- implemented electronic tax registration and created a centralized database,
- strengthened taxpayer services by disseminating information and raising

FIGURE 4.3
Tax Revenue, 2013–18

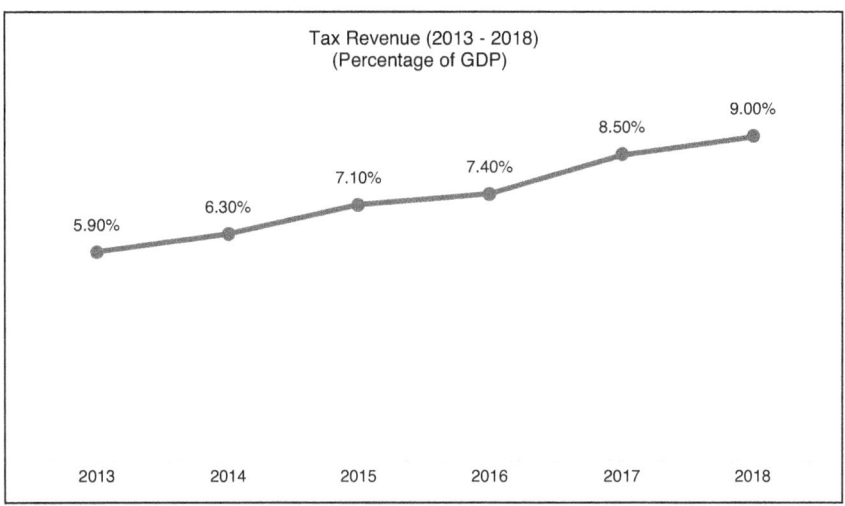

Source: Ministry of Economy and Finance, "Report on Monitoring and Evaluation of Implementing Revenue Mobilization Strategy 2014–2018" (2019).

awareness through workshops, education programs, advisory services and a call centre,
- launched single invoice and e-payment while creating additional banking tax payment options,
- developed and updated legal documents,
- built capacity of tax auditors in the use of electronic auditing management systems, and
- implemented debt repayment mechanisms, revised tax lawsuit rules and procedures, and established a tax dispute resolution committee.

Along with these important achievements, there was also recognition that a number of challenges, including tax evasion, lack of cooperation of small taxpayers, limited tax culture and certain organizational capacities. The expected result of the modernization is to improve operational efficiency, voluntary compliance, quality of service, and monitoring and evaluation mechanisms based on key performance indicators (KPIs).

Achieving key deliverables under the revenue mobilization strategy 2019–23 relies heavily on the modernization of core operating functions for processes and the further integration of tax administration. This includes the use of fully automated and integrated information technology systems across all core functions. In addition, it will also require strengthening the quality of taxpayer services, voluntary compliance, and the reduction of tax evasion.

The modernization of the internal support function is focused on interconnected tax administration information systems. This includes centralized data centres, taxpayer data, information systems, taxpayer service systems and institutional and inter-institutional data-sharing systems.

4.1.7 Non-Tax Revenue

Non-tax revenue includes revenue from the management, exploitation and sale of state properties, concessions, fees and charges derived from public services, fines and penalties, and other non-tax revenue. It includes fees earned from public service, state property leases, gaming activity and public enterprises.

Overall, MEF manages, monitors and enhances non-tax revenue through the General Department of State Property and Non-Tax Revenue and the General Department of Financial Industry. All revenue collected from the management of state properties is deposited into the National Treasury. Non-tax revenue accounts for an average of 19 per cent of the government's total revenue annually. It made up slightly more than 2.0 per cent of GDP during the period 2002–12. This form of revenue has been steadily increasing over the years to 2.8 per cent of GDP in 2018.

The implementation of the medium-term revenue mobilization strategy 2014–18 focused on the source of non-tax revenue and the system for managing non-tax revenue. In addition, the Non-Tax Revenue Management Information System (NRMIS) played an important role in the management of revenue from public service and state properties. It enabled a systemic recording and classification of revenue, reference documentation, and revenue report compilation. This system was put in place in 2018 in twenty-three line ministries and capital/provincial line departments in 2020.

Separately, a "State Asset Register Management Information System" (SARMIS) has been established to support a consistent and timely annual state asset inventory preparation. SARMIS was disseminated and operationalized in the first phase in LMs, capital/provincial administrations and other public entities in 2020. This phase allows the recording of four state asset types: land and building, machines, cars and motorcycles, and office equipment. Adding other types of state assets, such as infrastructure, to the database will be considered after 2023.

Overall, MEF has made the management of non-tax revenue more robust and complete. Major achievements include:

(1) Improved depositing and the recording of revenue to the National Treasury with wider use of the banking system.
(2) Strengthened the management of tourist admittance revenue to the Angkor site through the establishment of the Angkor Institution.
(3) The establishment of information technology systems for non-tax revenue management and state asset registration.
(4) The establishment and revision of a number of legal frameworks, including laws, royal decrees, sub-decrees, *Prakas* and circulars aimed at strengthening and effective management of non-tax revenue.

To contribute to achieving the 2030 vision of the RGC, the rollout of the revenue mobilization strategy 2019–23 was adopted. It aims to strengthen the non-tax administration and policy by focusing on information technology modernization for management and appropriate measures by sector to identify key revenue sources. This strategy will also focus on expanding the NRMIS which is set to offer online payment and mobile applications by 2022.

The revenue mobilization strategy 2019–23 is a governance tool to review and address the remaining challenges. It also further enhances the effectiveness of revenue management by introducing specific measures to modernize information systems, adopting necessary regulations and developing standards for management. These actions should increase revenue from sources such as civil aviation, tourism, mining and energy, and gambling activities.

4.1.8 Capital Revenue

Capital revenue is a non-recurring income. Capital revenue is planned by the MEF based on information derived from income from financial assets, debt and advance repayments by public enterprises, and borrowing in the local capital market. The MEF evaluates and analyses the economic situation and the issuance of bonds or government debt in other forms to estimate capital revenue from lending. Foreign financing, in the form of non-refundable financing for investment, is estimated based on the flow of funds and the progress of project implementation. Commodity funds in the form of goods are allocated to the revenue of the state budget with the expected amount under the program of importing such goods.

4.2 PUBLIC EXPENDITURE MANAGEMENT

Public expenditure management (PEM) aims at achieving three outcomes: aggregate fiscal discipline, allocative efficiency, and operational efficiency. Aggregate fiscal discipline refers to the alignment of public expenditures with total revenues. It means keeping government spending within sustainable limits, not spending more than what the government can afford. Allocative efficiency refers to the harmony of budgetary allocations with the strategic priorities of the country, or simply, spending money on the "right" things. Operational efficiency refers to the provision of public services at a reasonable quality and cost and value for the money.

Cambodia's 2008 Law on Public Financial Systems states that it is the obligation of the state to its people to ensure expenditure is based on the current needs and investment for the future. Hence, there are two types of expenditure: current expenditure and capital expenditure.

4.2.1 Current Expenditure

Cambodia's public finance has developed gradually since the early 1990s. The country moved to a free-market economy according to the 1993 constitutional law. In December 2004, RGC introduced the PFMRP to improve the national financial system. Domestic public revenue and public expenditure have since increased.

With strong economic growth, Cambodia moved from a low-income country to a lower middle-income status in 2015. With increased government revenue, spending has also increased significantly in the past few years. The increased expenditures are mainly absorbed by the MEF, Defence and Security, and Social Services. Despite increasing pressures due to the rising wages of civil servants and social security spending, the government has been trying to contain this spending to acceptable and prudent levels.

The public sector minimum wage was raised from KHR340,000 (US$85) in 2013 to more than KHR1 million (US$250) in 2018. This caused an increase in the overall public payroll, from 4.3 per cent of GDP in 2011 to 6.7 per cent in 2016. Wage spending as a share of government expenditure increased from around 20 per cent in 2010 to more than 30 per cent in 2016.

Another major challenge in current expenditure includes the lengthy processes that continue to hamper timely in-year budget disbursements, affecting the government agencies' ability to deliver quality public services. The government is rising to these challenges with the PFMRP by attracting skilled professionals into the civil service and introducing performance monitoring.

With assistance from the EU in 2020, major reforms in budgeting processes are underway, including the development of timelines for the LM Budget Strategic Plan (BSPs), annual budget schedules and medium-term capital expenditure schedules that will improve the timeliness of budget disbursement. These efforts will gradually assist in setting more realistic outcomes and output targets within a performance-informed budget system. Still, progress remains uneven, and further improvements are needed before program budgeting and BSPs can be considered fully effective.

4.2.2 Capital Expenditure

Capital expenditures are funds used by the government to acquire, upgrade, and maintain physical assets such as property, buildings, industrial plants, technology, transport infrastructure, water supply infrastructure, solid waste mechanisms or equipment. As shown in Figure 4.4, despite Cambodia's impressive economic growth, transportation infrastructure has not kept pace, and the quality of transportation lagged behind other ASEAN countries.

FIGURE 4.4
Comparison of Transportation Improvements

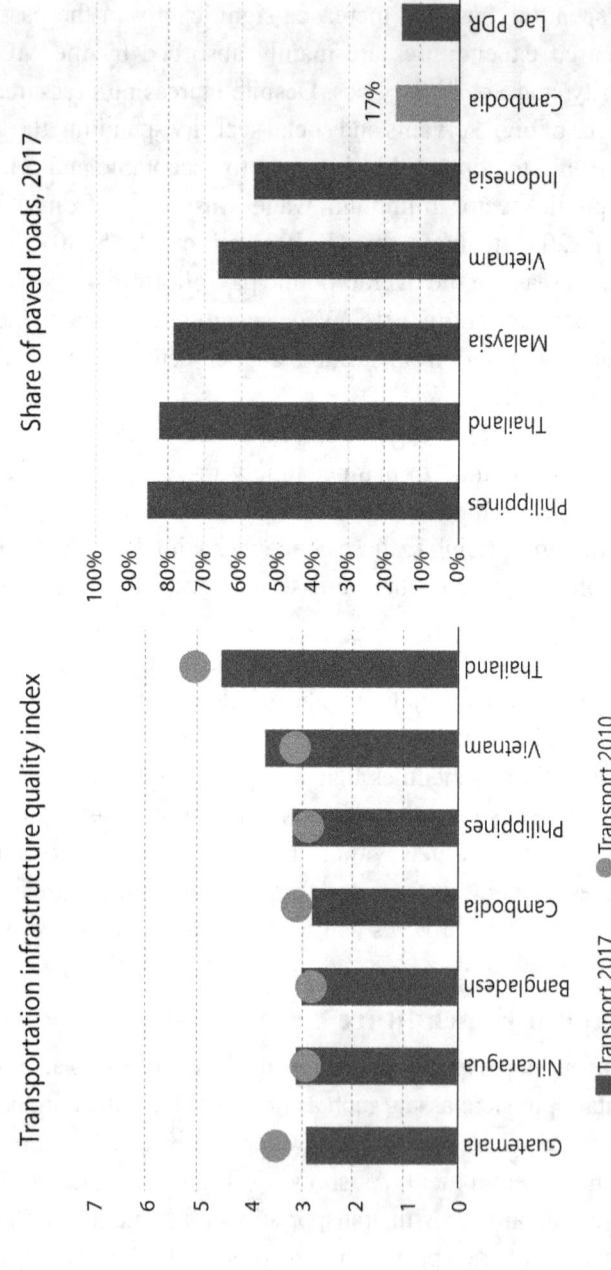

Source: World Economic Forum, Global Competitiveness Indicators, ASEAN statistics.

Road investment has traditionally received considerably more funding than education or health, with its peak at 4.3 per cent of GDP in 2012. In recent years, while investment in infrastructure remains a priority in government capital expenditure, investment in human resources development is becoming increasingly important, as reflected in government spending. Traditionally, infrastructure spending such as on roads and bridges is in the form of loans and grants from development partners especially from China and Japan, while the government allocates funds for operations and maintenance (O&M) (Figure 4.5).

The implementation of PFMRP has allowed Cambodia to modernize its public finance, with a key result of that being an increase in revenues. It, therefore, has provided the government with more opportunities for public infrastructure investments on its own, rather than relying on external funding. Cambodia's vision of becoming an upper-middle-income nation by 2030 and a high-income country by 2050 recognizes that infrastructure investments are key to making the country competitive in the region and achieving this vision.

4.3 PUBLIC INVESTMENT MANAGEMENT

Public investment refers to the expenditure on public infrastructure and is divided into two categories: economic infrastructures, such as roads, airports, and seaports, and social infrastructures, such as schools, hospitals, water supply, and sanitation. Public investment projects can be financed from a government's state budget, internal and external government borrowing, and possibly investment funds from the private sector. With a well-developed framework for public investment management (PIM), a government can get the maximum outputs and outcomes from public investment expenditure.

Public investment is also a government tool to boost economic growth in the long term. Designing a sound public investment system, therefore, will contribute to (1) supporting and stimulating sustainable economic growth while diversifying the economy and strengthening competitiveness; (2) fulfilling the need for increasing public investment funds; (3) ensuring that investment resources are used to meet government priorities; and (4) responding to public service demand. For PIM to succeed, Cambodia

FIGURE 4.5
Spending as a Percentage of GDP and National Budget

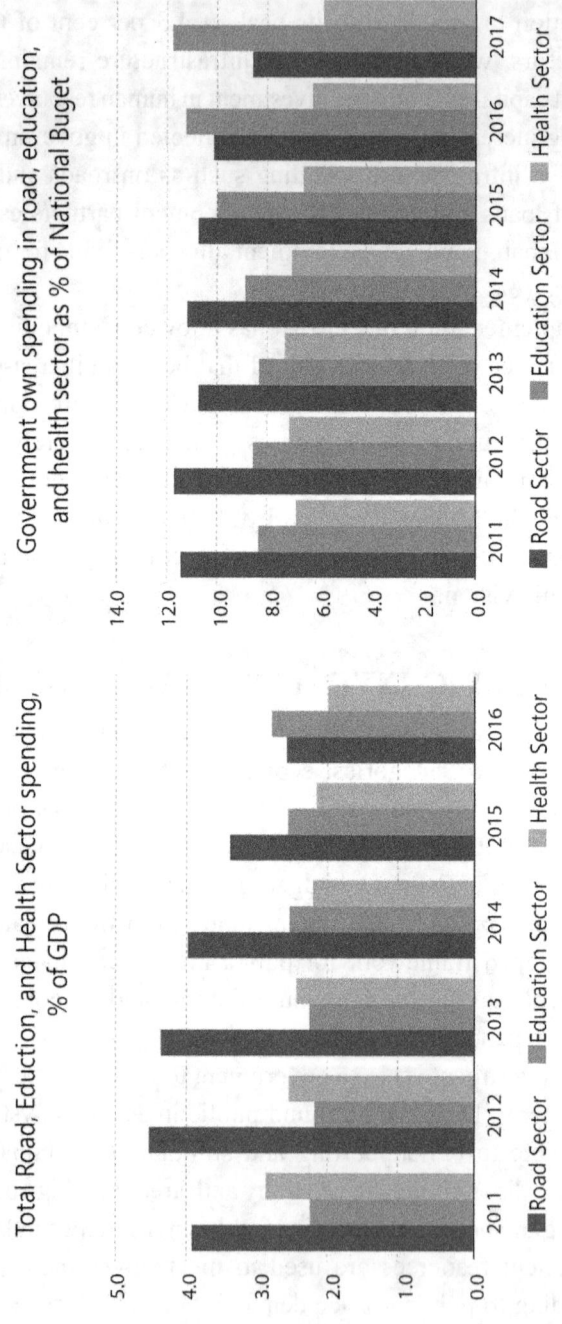

Source: National Treasury Database 2011–16, CDC DP Database 2011–16, and Sun-National Budget 2011–16.

will need an implementable policy framework, a legal framework, sound institutional arrangements, operational procedures, financial support mechanisms, and skilled human resources.

In Cambodia, there are several possible sources of funding for public investment projects: the national budget; a subnational government budget or their issuing of private securities; development partner funding; a public-private partnership; a public administrative establishment; and a state-owned enterprise. In some special cases, some public investment projects are conducted through the privatization of state assets, and joint funding between the government and private sector called "blended finance".

However, in Cambodia, there is no single legal or financial framework to control and manage public investment projects. In addition, there are no clear indicators as to whether all the approved projects are linked to government policies and priorities. Cambodia also faces the issue of integrating the capital and current budget processes. This has not been fully addressed in the PFMRP and has at times led to an insufficient budget for operation and maintenance after the completion of the projects.

To address this, the government adopted the Public Investment Management (PIM) System Reform Strategy 2019–25. The strategy aimed at developing an integrated national system for managing public investment from a variety of funding sources and at all levels of administration. The strategy's priority was to create a harmonized system for appraisal, prioritization, management, and monitoring of public investment. The government is gearing up its policies and procedures to govern PIM. After the PIM reform strategy was launched, various legal documents, such as one for public-private partnerships (PPPs) as an example, had to be developed; MEF also drafted a law on PPPs, which was adopted in 2021. Procurement procedures were created, and it is expected that "Standard Operational Procurements for PPP" will also be adopted soon.

Another priority of the strategy is to build capacity for relevant government officials in the area of PIM. The government is creating a capacity-building plan and a database to record the implementation of all projects, documenting both expenditure and progress.

At the end of 2019, the IMF made an assessment and developed some recommendations to strengthen PIM.

IMF's Recommendations for Improving Public Investment Management

Despite a significant effort to increase public investment over the past few decades, Cambodia still faces important infrastructure needs. Public investment has increased steadily since the early 1990s, gradually catching up with other Asian countries and converging at 8 per cent of GDP. Cambodia has also relied on public-private partnership (PPP) arrangements to develop economic infrastructure. As a result, access to electricity, education, and clean water has registered substantial progress. Yet, Cambodia still has one of the lowest public capital stocks per capita in the region. Extra investment in infrastructure will be necessary to fully achieve SDGs by 2030. Graduation to lower-middle-income status, which is expected to trigger a decrease in the share of concessional externally financed projects (currently still makes up about two-thirds of total public investment), will call for greater reliance on the national budget and on private sector participation to develop infrastructure.

Cambodia could get more infrastructure "bang for its buck" through stronger public investment management practices. In an environment with constrained resources, spending better is just as important as spending more on infrastructure. According to Fund staff calculations, the impact of Cambodia's public investment in terms of economic benefits (access and quality of infrastructure) is on average well below that of other countries in the region. This impact could be doubled through enhanced efficiency, which can be achieved by strengthening infrastructure governance.

The main shortcomings in infrastructure governance are mostly found downstream in the management cycle for domestically funded projects. Overall, while institutions to support infrastructure governance processes are in place, their effectiveness is hampered by fragmentation and limited coordination. The preparation of the capital budget is not based on individual projects. Rather, the capital budget is appropriated as lump sums and allocation to individual projects only occurs after the overall budget is approved, preventing coordination with the recurrent budget. Budget documents do not provide a comprehensive picture of all public investment projects. There is a need to improve the capacity to appraise and select projects through the development of in-house project quality assurance processes, to effectively measure project delays and cost overruns across the investment portfolio and improve in-year monitoring of individual projects at the level of line ministries.

Fabien Gonguet (FAD) based on findings of a recent 2019 PIMA mission

4.4 PUBLIC DEBT MANAGEMENT

Public debt is how much a country owes to lenders outside of itself. These lenders can include individuals, businesses, other governments, and multilateral and bilateral aid agencies. Public debt management is a method that allows the required amount of government funding to be raised in a manner consistent with government risk and cost objectives, and that addresses other debt management goals.

In 2019, RGC signed concessional loan agreements with development partners (DPs) for a total of US$504.65 million, which accounts for 36.0 per cent of its debt ceiling of SDR[1] of US$1,400 million. Overall, the loans are highly concessional with an average grant element of 55 per cent. Cumulatively, from 1993 to 2019, the RGC signed concessional loan agreements with DPs worth US$11.91 billion. Of those, 87.0 per cent was for infrastructure projects, and the remaining 13.0 per cent was for other priority sectors.

According to Cambodia's Strategy on Public Debt Management 2019–23, the loan policy is guided by four principles. The strategy seeks to keep a certain ratio of credit to the scale of the economy and budget; the credit must have a low interest rate and be highly concessional; the government will only borrow for priority sectors that have high growth and productivity potential; and the loans will be used transparently, accountably, efficiently and effectively.

Official development assistance (ODA) has been the main source of finance for Cambodia's public investment. As Cambodia's international status improves, it will see a reduction of access to grants and slight interest rate increases on concessional loans. The decrease in grant aid is a common trend when a country's economic status improves from "low income" to a more advanced economy. As international terms aid change, externally funded public investment, both social and economic infrastructure, may decrease.

Finally, in the future, development financing will require greater collaboration from different government institutions towards a common goal of resource mobilization. This will necessitate well-coordinated policies and the institutional rearrangement of the development administration in the future. The government should consider a more expansive internal financing strategy, such as developing and leveraging government bonds in the domestic bond market and raising public awareness of the importance of the bond market for Cambodia's sustainable growth. In short, managing internal and external debt in the country is necessary for Cambodia to reduce risk and develop its financial sector as a whole.

4.5 STATE PROPERTY MANAGEMENT

There is no clear definition of state property in the laws promulgated to date in Cambodia, though several laws describe how it will be regulated. MEF establishes policies, laws and regulations to manage state property, both at the national and subnational levels. MEF reviews and approves all state properties' management contracts and state concession grants related to public finance. All revenues resulting from the operation and management of state properties are paid into the National Treasury.

The RGC has made significant progress on state property management. The General Department of State Property and Non-Tax Revenue (GDSPNR) of the MEF has prepared a draft of an inventory book of state property. It has launched a *Prakas* detailing measures and procedures for clearing the inventory of state property. In addition, GDSPNR developed a State Asset Register Management Information System (SARMIS) that is connected with all holding authorities across the country. The system is administered at two levels: by MEF as the managing authority and by LMs or subnational administrations as the holding authority.

In the past, the absence of a law on the management of state property posed challenges to the management and control of state property, especially when it came to the classification of state property, setting fees, inventory management, transfer of ownership, conservation, and development. The *Prakas* and SARMIS provide a clear and specific legal framework, which was lacking in the past, for the management of state property. These steps are key for setting up a transparent environment for state property management, which has been ambiguous for a long time. Adoption of these new tools will help the government better manage and control state property and to collect revenue from this source more efficiently.

4.6 PUBLIC PROCUREMENT MANAGEMENT

Public procurement is an expenditure mechanism that governments use to acquire goods and services from the market to support public projects and everyday government activities. Sound public procurement ensures that government budget execution is efficient and effective, achieving the highest value for money. Governments around the world spend an estimated US$9.5 trillion in public contracts every year, which in many developing countries represents 15–22 per cent of GDP (Procurement for Development, worldbank.org). From building roads and power stations to purchasing pharmaceuticals and securing trash collection services, efficient use of public resources contributes to better delivery of services.

Given these large amounts of money, governments need to keep a careful eye on the procedures, approaches and institutional arrangements involved in public procurement. Therefore, proper laws and legal frameworks should be in place and effectively implemented.

Key elements of public procurement are a viable procurement plan, monitoring and evaluation procedures, and complaint-handling mechanisms. To ensure these elements are achieved in a transparent and effective public procurement process, clearly defined roles for regulators, implementers, and an oversight body are needed.

In Cambodia, MEF is the procurement regulator and is responsible for developing policies and a legal framework, training procurement agents, conducting procurement audits and handling complaints and procurement disputes. Line ministries are the public procurement implementers who implement public procurement processes.

Depending on the value and type of procurement, MEF will assume the oversight role through its representation on the Procurement Review Committee (PRC). MEF has set different thresholds for decision-making on procurement for different government agencies. If the procurement does not meet MEF's threshold, no further approval is needed from the ministry. Any single sourcing, direct contracting or force account procurement requires prior approval from the MEF.

The public procurement system in Cambodia was evaluated by the PEFA[2] in 2015 and 2020 as well as by the ADB in 2015 using OECD indicators. The evaluation results showed a significant improvement in some areas of the procurement system. However, opportunities for reform in many of the key elements of the system were found, including institutional framework and management capacity, procurement operation and market practice, transparency, and the complaints handling mechanism.

Moreover, the evaluation found fragmentation in the legal framework for the procurement of national budgets and donor funds.

In response to these findings, the government has introduced the public procurement system reform strategy 2019–25 which is aligned with Budget System Reform Strategy (BSRS) 2018–25, aiming to strengthen accountability mechanisms in public procurement practices. Included in the strategy are the identified and defined roles of the regulator, implementer and oversight body. Procurement decentralization is also an important agenda in the reform. The authority and right to make decisions are gradually given to the procurement entities at line ministries to procure goods and services. Meanwhile, MEF will strengthen the procurement audit, covering all sources of funds including externally funded and state budgets and focusing more on outputs and results. The Independent Complaints Handling Mechanism will be improved with the inclusion of a sanction regime.

The government is also considering creating electronic government procurement (e-GP) to ensure a more transparent, timely and effective procurement process. This will attempt to solve the problem of incomplete information management and lengthy procedures. The procurement function will be added to the FMIS system, and e-GP will be conducted within that system.

4.7 PUBLIC ACCOUNTING SYSTEM

Public Sector Accounting in Cambodia is a mixture of accrual and cash accounting with many transactions recorded on an accrual basis. The previous Chart of Accounts (COA)—the list used by a government that identifies each item for which money or the equivalent is spent or received—was originally based on the French accounting system which, over time, was adapted to reflect the RGCs accounting requirements and practices. It was not designed to handle both accruals- and cash-based accounting to facilitate the implementation of an accrual-based system or produce accrual-based reports.

The categories of the previous COA were different from those used by the International Public Sector Accounting Standards (IPSAS) and International Financial Reporting Standards (IFRSs), making it difficult for accountants outside the Cambodian public sector to use or understand them. In addition, the COA was crowded, which meant that classification numbers were restrictive, forcing heavy use of accounts labelled "others". This rendered it practically impossible to track many expenditures or liabilities.

In 2012, the RGC adopted IPSAS accounting and reporting standards and agreed to meet the requirements under cash-based IPSAS. This led to a gradual transition over time to accrual-based standards. Cambodia joined many governments around the world in using these standards to prepare their financial statements. In doing so, the RGC expressed its commitment to improving the consistency, quality, and transparency of its accounting and reporting policies and standards. Adopting IPSAS and achieving compliance with IPSAS would create a high level of confidence in government financial reporting quality and increase the relevance and reliability of financial information.

Cambodia's public sector accounting was different from the IPSAS in three major areas. First, IPSAS requires that financial statements include a statement of financial position, a statement of financial performance, a cash flow statement, a statement of changes in net assets, a budget comparison, and notes. The Cambodian public financial reporting, the budget execution law, includes only a statement of revenues and statements of expense and expenditure. The government is moving to modify the budget execution law to produce a complete set of financial statements and the French Government is providing technical assistance towards this end.

The second key difference is that IPSAS requires that financial information for all controlled entities be consolidated in the financial statements. Cambodian financial reporting excludes significant controlled entities, such as hospitals and state-owned enterprises. IPSAS also requires that transactions between controlled entities be eliminated so that revenue and expenses are not overstated. However, the Cambodian financial reports do not eliminate these transactions.

The third main difference is that IPSAS requires financial information incorporated in the financial statements to be prepared with uniform accounting policies. Unfortunately, a significant portion of government spending does not follow the accounting policies and procedures set by the General Department of National Treasury (GDNT), Cambodia's public accounting body.

The RGC is increasingly concerned about financial accountability and transparency, data and information sharing with citizens and stakeholders, and efficiency and effectiveness in the use of resources for public services. Cash-based accounting has been shown to have many weaknesses as transactions are only recognized when cash is physically paid or received, neglecting the corresponding economic transactions' timing or the term benefits of the transactions.

Internationally, the public sector is attempting to follow the accounting standards that private sector companies have used for many years and IPSAS is the public sector equivalent of those accounting standards. The adoption of IPSAS has allowed the RGC to introduce private sector techniques and skills into their financial management. As a result, the quality and depth of financial data and information available to the government have greatly enhanced the quality of financial reports and statements.

Following the milestones included in the Budget System Reform Strategy (BSRS) 2018–25, the National Accounting Council (NAC) has developed a roadmap shifting from cash-basis to accrual-basis accounting. Figure 4.6 shows the timelines for standards to be applied, corresponding with IPSAS implementation.

National Accounting Council

The National Accounting Council (NAC) is the regulator of the RGC that oversees the accounting and auditing profession in Cambodia. Under the Cambodian Public Sector Accounting Standards (CPSAS), the NAC is responsible for preparing, updating and approving drafts of accounting standards for the government's use. It also promotes the implementation of Cambodian public accounting standards to ensure financial accountability, transparency, and good governance in Cambodia.

The RGC recently launched the Cash Basis CPSAS (CB CPSAS). To strengthen the capacity of implementers as well as raise awareness, NAC has conducted training of the CB CPSAS to GDNT staff and relevant staff within the RGC.

General Department of National Treasury

The General Department of the National Treasury (GDNT) is the government's only public entity to implement Cambodia's public accounting

FIGURE 4.6
Timeline for the Development of Accrual-Based Accounting

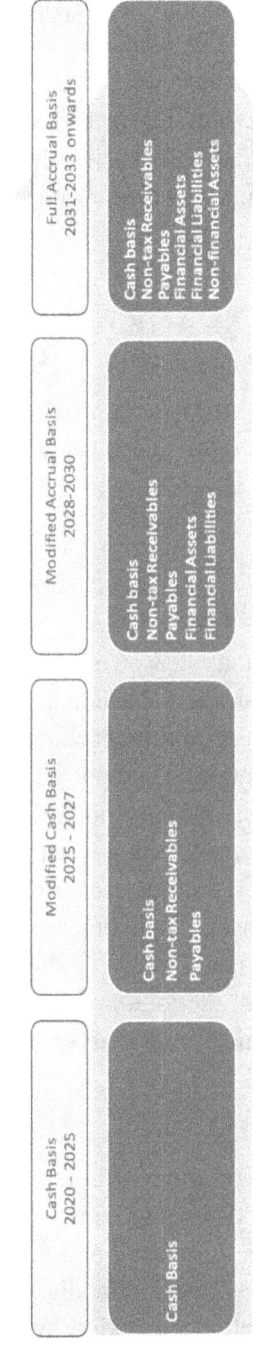

Source: Strategy on Implementing Accrual Basis Cambodian Public Sector Accounting Standards 2021–31 (2022).

principles and regulations. The GDNT prepares the financial statements under the Cash Basis IPSAS. Efforts to finalize the National Government General Purpose Financial Statements for 2017, 2018 and 2019 are well advanced and increasingly compliant with IPSAS standards.

Supported by international IPSAS specialists, the published financial statements have improved each year towards meeting international standard disclosures and presentations.

4.8 FINANCIAL MANAGEMENT INFORMATION SYSTEM (FMIS)

The second stage of the PFMRP for "improving financial accountability" was launched in 2008. Within this second stage, a Financial Management Information System (FMIS) was formed as a core element to fully support PFMRP.

4.8.1 Overview of FMIS

Financial Management Information Systems (FMIS) support the automation and integration of public financial management processes including budget formulation, execution (e.g., commitment control, cash/debt management, treasury operations), accounting and reporting. A financial management system will produce certain outputs, including operating and capital budgets, accounting reports, working capital reports, forecasts of cash flows, and analyses based on various scenarios. The financial data itself may be analysed in multiple ways, including trend evaluation, ratio analysis and financial modelling. When all these applications exist as modules in the same overall application, then the system is known as an integrated financial management information system or FMIS.

4.8.2 Objective of FMIS

The overarching objective of the FMIS implementation is to support and underpin the general PFMRP activities in all stages by improving accountability, effectiveness, efficiency and modernization of the public financial management system in Cambodia. This will provide timely and comprehensive information on budget revenue and expenditure in the medium and longer term. The FMIS will provide automated support (turnkey solution) to budget planning and formulation and the budget execution processes, with a stronger system and reinforced controls.

4.8.3 Benefits of FMIS

FMIS is a tool for automating all manual PFM processes into a fully integrated PFM system covering budget formulation, budget implementation, accounting, reporting, monitoring and auditing (Figure 4.7). It covers more than software and hardware; it includes people, organization and managing changes, and in those respects, brings about new business processes. The immediate benefits of FMIS are the improvement of budget execution through streamlined and automated payments, revenue-receiving (collection and remittance for Non-Tax and links to Tax, Customs and Debt Management systems), and accounting and reporting in the Central and

FIGURE 4.7
FMIS System Outline

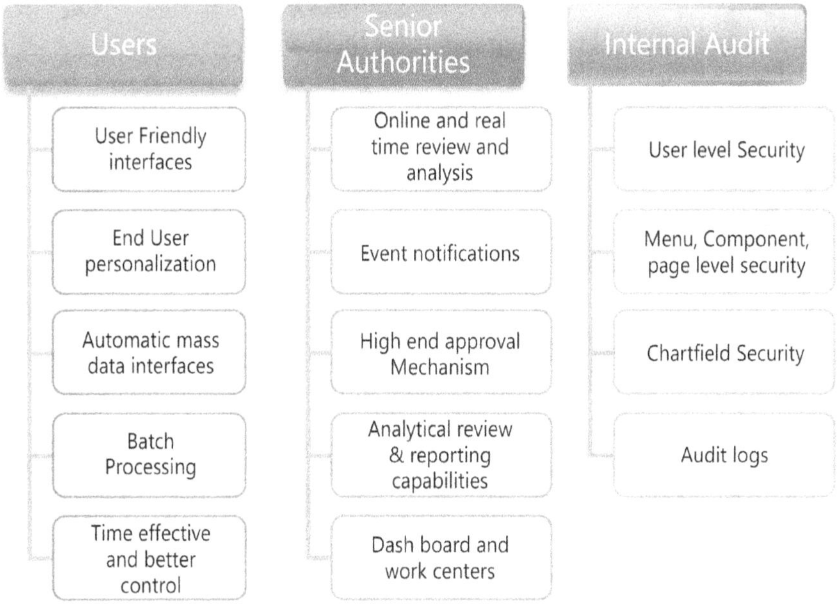

Users	Senior Authorities	Internal Audit
User Friendly interfaces	Online and real time review and analysis	User level Security
End User personalization	Event notifications	Menu, Component, page level security
Automatic mass data interfaces	High end approval Mechanism	Chartfield Security
Batch Processing	Analytical review & reporting capabilities	Audit logs
Time effective and better control	Dash board and work centers	

Source: FMIS (2016), fmis.mef.gov.kh: https://fmis.mef.gov.kh/contents/uploads/2016/07/Benefit.png

Provincial Treasuries. Providing transparent online access to all financial information will also help improve PFM. Besides this, FMIS provides an opportunity to implement best practices that follow the international standard of financial management for the government. Before 2025, Cambodia will have a robust FMIS system to decentralize the management and budget implementation to line ministries and to evaluate results.

4.8.4 Core Modules and Interfacing of FMIS

There are six core modules in the current FMIS, including Budget Allocation (BA), Accounts Receivable (AR), Accounts Payable (AP), Cash Management (CM), Purchase Order (PO) and General Ledger (GL) Two additional modules, Budget Planning and Procurement, were planned to be developed and piloted in 2020 and eventually rolled out to all line ministries starting in 2021. In addition, FMIS also consists of seven budget classifications that allow reports to be exported and categorized accordingly. Figure 4.8 illustrates the modules of FMIS and the interface of FMIS with other systems like the bank system, ASYCUDA, DMFAS, NRMIS, Tax and Payroll. It also illustrates how the FIMS system interfaces with other systems and easily generates reports for the users.

This section describes these eight modules and seven budget classifications as well as how they interact with other systems to facilitate the government's financial transactions and reporting.

(a) FMIS' Six Core Modules

Budget Allocation (BA) Module has three main operations: budget law entry, adding credit, and adjusting credit for line ministries making internal adjustments (Figure 4.9). The Budget Allocation Module records the budget law of line ministries, departments under line ministries, and budget entities at the subnational level.

Accounts Receivable (AR) Module records revenue transactions, such as temporary revenue from banks, transfer temporary revenue from across entities and records revenue of the GDNT and provincial treasuries (including refunds and deposits to customers) (Figure 4.10).

Accounts Payable (AP) Module records the expenditure operations of line ministries and budget entities, including direct payments, procurement

FIGURE 4.8
Modelling for FMIS and Interfacing

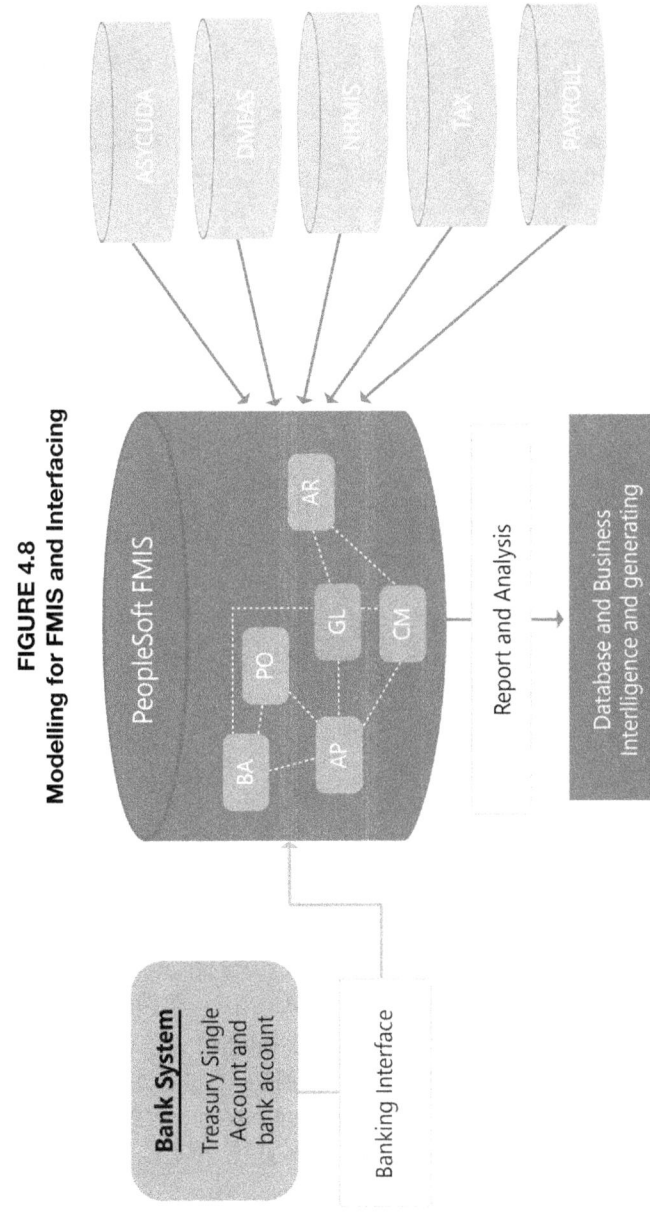

Source: Cambodia Public Financial Management Manual (2023).

FIGURE 4.9
Overview of Budget Allocation Module

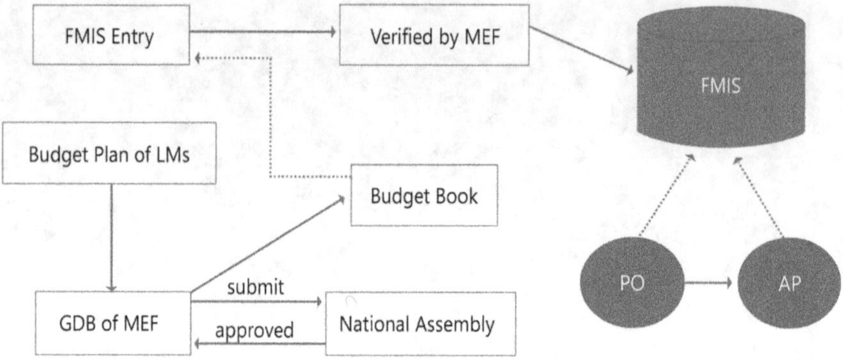

Source: Cambodia Public Financial Management Manual (2023).

FIGURE 4.10
Overview of Workflow for Accounts Receivable

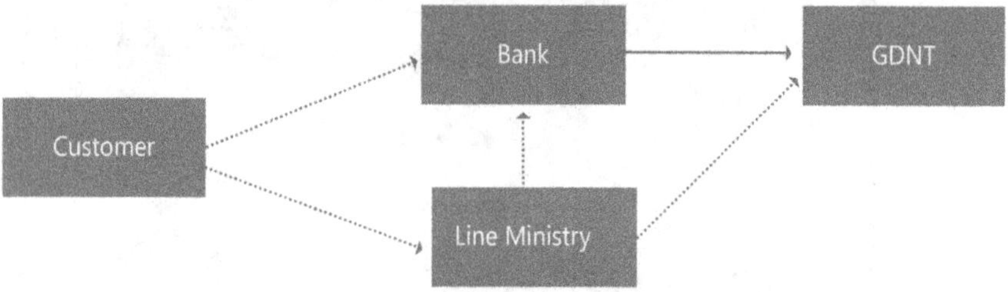

Source: Cambodia Public Financial Management Manual (2023).

payments, vouchers for advance clearance/petty cash, and general expenses (Figure 4.11). AR has four main functions: record voucher/advance, advance commitment, end date process, and data maintenance.

Cash Management (CA) Module records and checks cash/balance. It has four main functions: (1) bank account maintenance, (2) budget transfer, (3) bank statement, and (4) accounting entry (Figure 4.12). It is linked with other FMIS Modules, including Revenue, Expense and General Ledger. CA can record balance transfers from one bank account to another, interface bank statements automatically, and verify the transactions of revenues,

FIGURE 4.11
Overview of Workflow for Accounts Payable

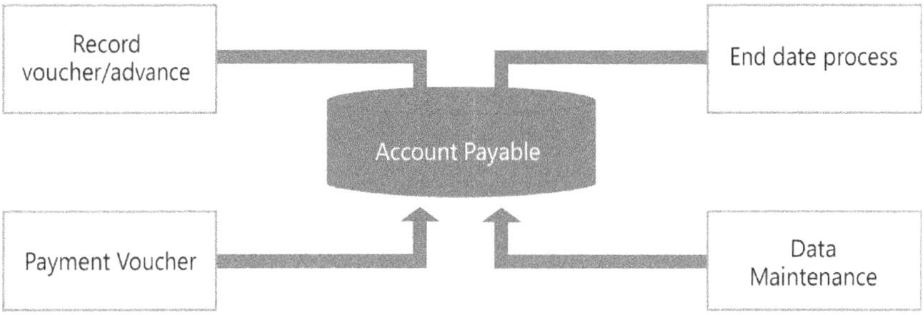

```
┌─────────────────┐                              ┌─────────────────┐
│     Record      │                              │                 │
│ voucher/advance ├──────────┐        ┌──────────┤ End date process│
└─────────────────┘          │        │          └─────────────────┘
                         ╔═══╧════════╧═══╗
                         ║ Account Payable ║
                         ╚═══╤════════╤═══╝
                             ▲        ▲
┌─────────────────┐          │        │          ┌─────────────────┐
│                 │          │        │          │      Data       │
│ Payment Voucher ├──────────┘        └──────────┤   Maintenance   │
└─────────────────┘                              └─────────────────┘
```

Source: Cambodia Public Financial Management Manual (2023).

expenses, and transfers with bank statements. CA is currently implemented at GDNT and capital-provincial treasuries.

Purchase Order (PO) Module records transactions in FMIS, including requisition and any operation relevant to purchasing services and goods (Figure 4.13).

General Ledger (GL) Module is a primary core module of the FMIS that creates and controls master data—the budget classification (Figure 4.14). It sets rules for transactions, records account open and closing dates, allows the creation, modification, approval request, approval, copy and deletion of journals, verifies financial information, queries account receivables, accounts payables, cash management, and calculates profits and losses from exchange rates before and during the closing of the annual accounts. The GL is used only by the Accounting Department of GDNT and the accounting offices of capital-provincial treasuries.

These six core modules are linked to or interfaced with other systems, including private banks, the Debt Management and Financial Analysis System (DMFAS), the Automated System for Customs Data (ASYCUDA), the Non-Tax Revenue Management Information System (NRMIS), the payroll system, the Tax System, and the National Bank of Cambodia's Electronic Fund Transfer (EFT).

EFT is a function in FMIS that allows electronic payments to suppliers or line ministries. It eliminates the need for the suppliers or line ministries to be physically present at the General Department of National Treasury

Components of PFM in Cambodia • 87

FIGURE 4.12
Overview of Cash Management

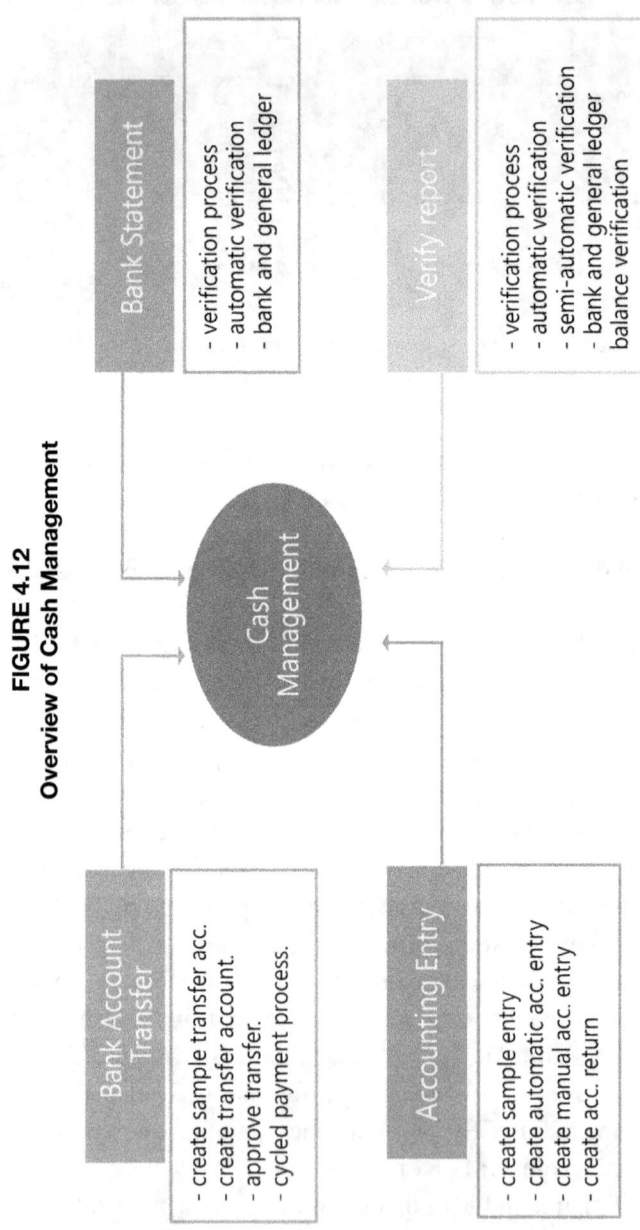

Source: Cambodia Public Financial Management Manual (2023).

FIGURE 4.13
Overview of Purchase Order

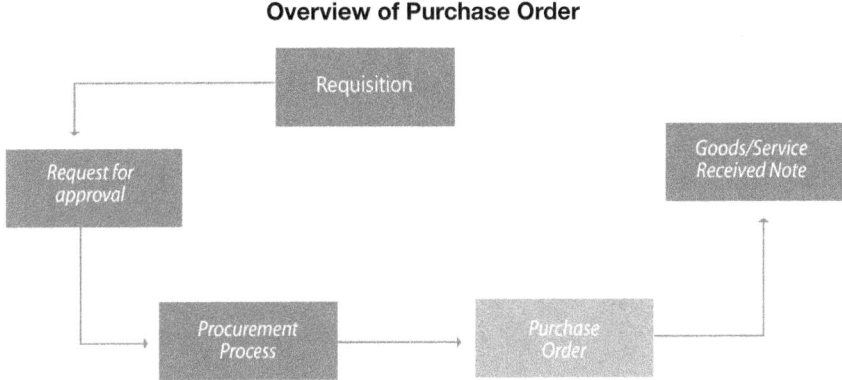

Source: Cambodia Public Financial Management Manual (2023).

or Municipal-Provincial Treasury to receive payments. GDNT transfers the payment from the TSA account directly to the bank account of the supplier or line ministry.

The current six FMIS modules do not fully meet the requirements of public financial management and some tasks are still processed manually. The FMIS Budget Allocation Module is currently used to record the budget law approved by the National Assembly.

(b) Two Additional Modules Are Planned to Be Developed, Piloted and Rolled Out

Because budget planning processes are still being done manually, two additional FMIS modules, Budget Planning and Procurement, were initiated to be developed to enable line ministries to plan their annual expenditures and revenues in the system. The modules have been successfully developed and piloted in two line ministries during mid-2021, namely the MEF and the Ministry of Women's Affairs and subsequently to all LMs.

Budget Planning Module (BP) Module will enable line ministries and budget entities to plan annual expenditures and revenues and to conduct negotiations via the FMIS system instead of manually. Expanding the implementation of the BP module will save time in checking and adjusting the proposed budget of line ministries. Moreover, line ministries and budget entities will be able to see and keep track of the budget adjustments done by the GDB of MEF.

Components of PFM in Cambodia • 89

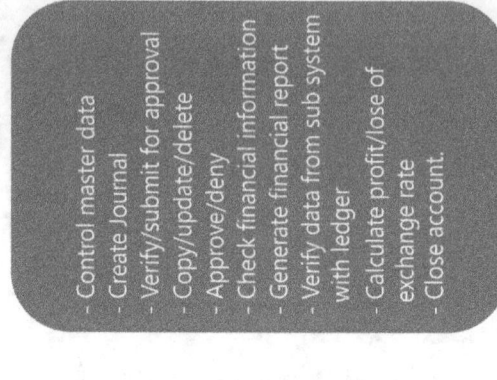

**FIGURE 4.14
Overview of General Ledger**

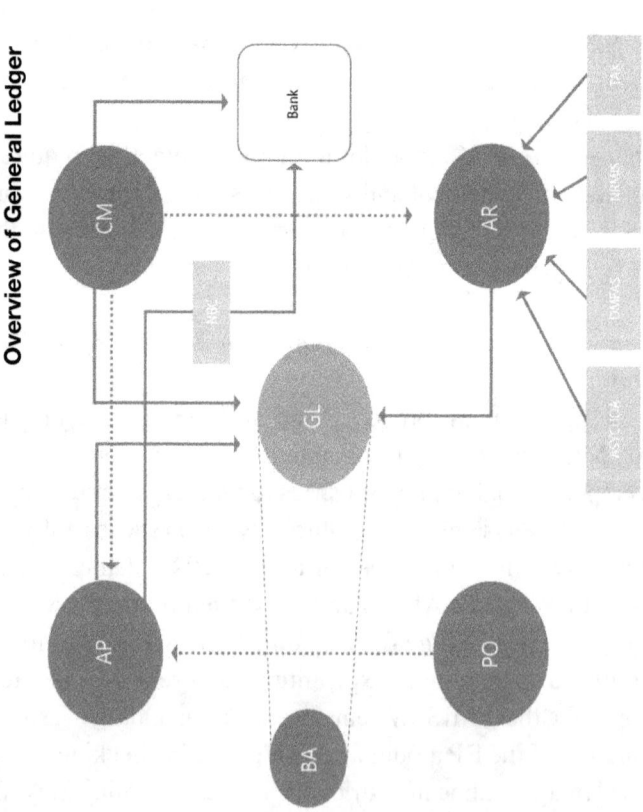

Source: Cambodia Public Financial Management Manual (2023).

Procurement Module. The current FMIS only records limited data in the public procurement process, maintaining only data on contracts and the delivery and receipt of goods and services. This data limitation poses a major challenge to the effective monitoring and managing of information. The planned Procurement Module will enable the recording of all relevant information and data at every step of the public procurement process: the preparation of procurement plans, the preparation of the required documents for bidding, advertising for goods and services, management of bidders, management of the bidding process, tracking of contract delivery, management of contracts, and management of the delivery, all the way to when goods and services are received.

(c) Seven Budget Classifications

In addition to the core modules, seven budget classifications, including economic, administrative, functional, geographical, program, source of funding, and project classification were designed in FMIS (Figure 4.15). Budget execution, expenditure, and revenue reports at national and subnational entities can be extracted from the FMIS system by these seven budget classifications and charts of accounts.

4.8.5 FMIS Implementation

MEF set out a three-phase implementation of FMIS. Phase 1 was to implement only the main treasury function that enables budgeting and commitment. In this phase, the FMIS was operationalized by MEF's key general departments.

In Phase 2, FMIS was rolled out to all thirty-seven line ministries, twenty-five capital-provincial departments of MEF, and other authorized budget entities and agencies of the RGC. The extended system covers additional modules, such as Budget Planning and Formulation and Procurement.

A detailed action plan for FMIS Phase 3 (2021–25) was adopted for implementation in 2021. This phase will see FMIS core functions extended to twenty-five municipal provincial administrations, priority departments of line ministries, new central and local budget entities, and public administration entities (PAEs).

FIGURE 4.15
Seven Budget Classifications

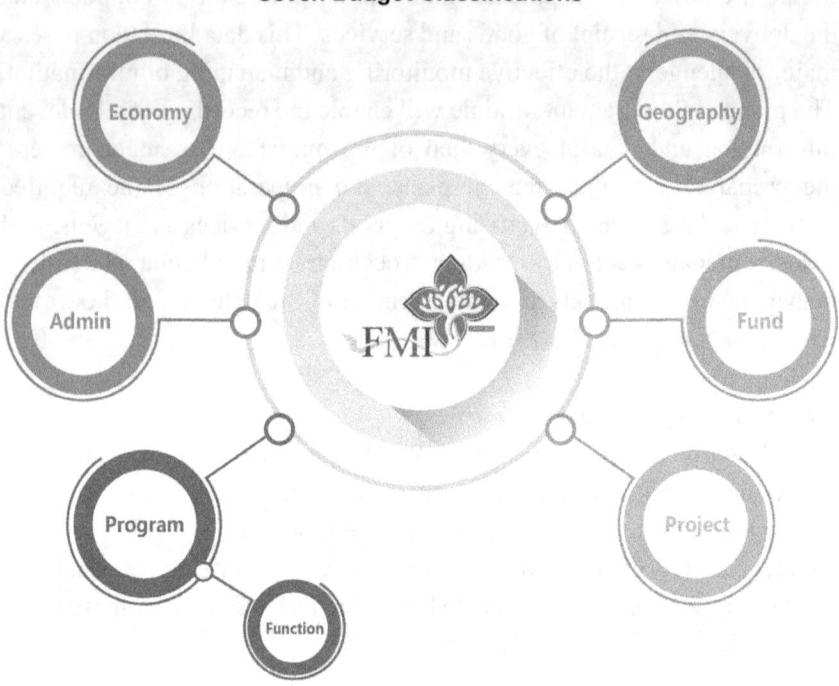

Source: Cambodia PFMRP Bulletin no. 6 (2019).

MEF spent eighteen months between December 2013 and 30 June 2015 developing the basis of FMIS. Phase 1 of FMIS was rolled out in three steps, deploying six core functions to seven general departments and twenty-five provincial and municipal treasures. The seven key general departments in which the six core functions were deployed are the General Department of National Treasury, the General Department of Budget, the General Department of International Cooperation and Debt Management, the General Department of Public Procurement, the General Department of Subnational Administration Finance, General Department of Internal Audit, and the General Department of Inspection.

With the Phase 1 FMIS rollout completed, the working group of FMIS turned its attention to Phase 2 (2017–21). During the course of four years, FMIS is to be deployed to all thirty-seven line ministries and twenty-five departments of the MEF. As of 2020, FMIS was operationalized in all line ministries and capital-provincial Departments of Economy and Finance.

The FMIS blueprint Phase 3 (2021–25) has been approved by the MEF's Management in 2021, covering the expansion of implementing core modules to the twenty-five capital/provincial administrations, all priority line departments, the fully authorized budget entities at the central level, new local levels, and public entities, expanding the implementation of budget planning and procurement modules at all LMs, and further planning and development of state asset and inventory management modules in FMIS.

4.8.6 Business Process Streamlining

Although FMIS is designed to provide many of the features and advantages described above, the system is still considered an additional workload for users because some tasks are still processed both manually and in the FMIS system. To fully automate all processes, parallel processes outside of the FMIS system need to be removed and/or fully integrated into the system. To achieve this, the Financial Management Work Group developed the Strategic Plan on Streamlining Business Process 2020–25. The strategy was adopted in the PFMRC meeting on 16 March 2020.

The strategy aims to systematically and fully integrate all business processes related to public financial management that are currently processed manually into the FMIS system. The purpose is to enable more transparency, accountability, efficiency and effectiveness. The strategy identifies the business process of settling low-risk expenditure (wage and direct payments) and covering higher-risk recurrent expenditure. The business processes are classified into four categories: (1) commitments and payments, (2) budget movement, (3) revenue execution, and (4) public procurement.

In the first year of implementation (2020), new business processes for the payment of salaries and expenses for staff have been formally operationalized in MEF and seven other LMs. The lessons learnt from these eight ministries will be the basis to roll out business processes to other LMs as well as the capital/provincial administrations.

4.8.7 Change Management

Change management is an important catalyst to implement FMIS successfully. Change management is the process of helping people understand the need for change and to motivate them to take actions that result in sustained changes in behaviour. It is different from project management or systems design in that it focuses less on the technical side of reform than on the behaviour of people. A central tenet of change management is the idea that organizations must frequently change in response to pressures from the external environment, including the availability of new technology, the emergence of new problems, or the threat of external competition. Change management consists of five important elements: (1) compiling the case for changes, (2) stakeholder analysis, (3) change readiness assessment, (4) communications plan, and (5) follow-up and sustainability.

An action plan for change management has been formulated through the ADKAR model (Awareness–Desire–Knowledge–Ability–Reinforcement). The goals are to change FMIS users from being recipients of change to being change-makers, to change FMIS from being just a recording and accounting system to a system used to manage, monitor and analyse the program and budget implementation, and to change the business process from manual, isolated and unconnected systems to a complete FMIS system. In 2020, FMWG introduced Change Management Plan for the FMIS project. The plan shows clearly that change management is crucial to transform the existing business process into one that is simple, efficient, and accountable. The objectives are to (1) study and analyse the current business processes that need to be revised, (2) prepare the relevant people supporting change, (3) analyse the impact and implementation mechanisms to minimize the negative impact on relevant people, and (4) formulate mechanisms to ensure sustainability after the change.

4.9 CONTROL SYSTEMS

4.9.1 Internal Audit and Financial Inspection System

Both internal auditors and inspectors are civil servants that are part of every government ministry and agency. They play an important role in examining internal controls and recommending better ways of processing and reducing financial risk—both mistakes and deliberate fraud—present in all government financial dealings.

Internal Audit

"Internal auditing is an independent, objective assurance and consulting activity designed to add value and improve an organization's operations. It helps an organization accomplish its objectives by bringing a systematic, disciplined approach to evaluate and improve the effectiveness of risk management, control, and governance processes."[3] The objective of an internal audit is to assist members of the organization to effectively discharge their responsibilities. To this end, internal auditing furnishes them with analyses, appraisals, recommendations, counsel, and information concerning the activities reviewed.

In Cambodia, internal audit departments carry out their quality control and risk management functions by reviewing and evaluating the activities of departments under their purview. Auditors must determine the appropriateness and adequacy of the entity's internal control system, and the integrity of financial and operating data, to assure that the existing systems comply with relevant policies, legal procedures and other regulations on operating and reporting. When institutions, ministries and public enterprises fail to implement programs according to existing policies, procedures, and regulations, it is necessary to recommend changes and improvements.

Along with compliance, auditors also look at the efficiency of resource usage and the completion of work plans and objectives. By participating in the planning and development of systems, particularly IT systems, the auditors can determine whether user needs are met, necessary controls are in place, and documentation is complete and accurate. Post-instalment evaluations of IT systems help to assure that systems can carry out their intended purposes.

Fraud prevention and staff compliance with codes of conduct are key outcomes of audit reviews.

The internal audit department reports its findings to top personnel in the ministries and agencies of the RGC, and the National Audit Authority. This allows senior managers to take the necessary actions to correct identified problems. Auditors also follow up on their recommendations to determine if adequate steps have been taken by the relevant managers.

Inspection

Financial inspection is carried out on the instructions of a line minister to investigate fraud, graft, and financial misappropriation. Each Ministry has its Inspection Unit and it is directed by and reports directly to the minister.

An inspection department generally reports directly to a minister on a confidential basis. It is typically carried out based on a specific complaint from a source within an entity, that is, information from a staff person within the organization. It is also used to determine if a person complies with regulations or if their activities are in violation to the extent of misuse of public resources and criminal actions. The inspection can be any special investigation of a specific individual through visits and review of documents, facilities and records, which can then be used as supporting pieces of evidence. The report and evaluation follow such visits.

The inspection is an assessment at a "moment in time" which identifies positive and adverse conditions. It is carried out through extensive physical examination of a facility and its equipment and is an observation of practices to collect information to determine compliance of a specific group or individual. The inspection function is more or less similar to an investigation by police. In the usual practice, it is done in response to any irregular act of an individual in the organization, who may be involved in a misuse of public resources, fraud and corruption, or violation of their provided authorities and power. Reports are generally not disclosed to the public, unlike audit reports.

4.9.2 Independent Audit

The independent and professional Supreme Audit Institution (SAI) is an important factor in a country's accountability chain. The Law of Audit of the RGC, enacted and implemented in March 2000, established the National Audit Authority (NAA) and the role of internal audit. The NAA is an independent, public entity and reports directly to the National Assembly, the Senate and the Government.[4] The Auditor-General (AG) and Deputy Auditor General (DAG) are appointed by a Royal Decree based on the government's recommendation and approved by a two-thirds majority vote in the National Assembly. The appointment term is five years, and the AG and DAG are eligible to be reappointed for one additional five-year term only. NAA has vast information-gathering powers to access the operational information of public organizations and entities. To audit the NAA itself, the Economic, Finance, Banking and Auditing Committee of the National Assembly could select an independent auditor to review the activities and operations of the NAA.

By law and current practice, the NAA has to review the Document of Settlement of the annual budget in parallel with the request of the National Assembly and with Senate examination and approval. The NAA has to certify the statement in the settlement document. However, if the MEF fails to share the settlement document within nine months after the closing of the fiscal year, the NAA will report this to the Nation Assembly and Senate. If serious issues occur, the Auditor-General can immediately bring them to the National Assembly's and Senate's attention.

To support the PFMRP agenda of RGC, the NAA has played an active role in developing supporting legal documents related to the audit work. Three types of audits are currently practised: (1) compliance audits, (2) financial audits, and (3) performance audits. The supporting guidelines on each type of audit are prepared and available.

A performance audit is generally a newly adopted practice in some countries. It is a supporting factor in promoting performance-informed budgeting. The main objective of conducting a performance audit is to enhance economy, effectiveness and efficiency in governance. Moreover, the performance audit improves transparency that helps the National Assembly, taxpayers and DPs to gain more understanding of the resources being utilized in the performance of government activities. To ensure effective and efficient oversight and internal control function, the Supreme Audit Institution and Internal Audit units maintain close coordination, cooperation, and regular communication.

4.10 SUMMARY

This chapter describes in detail each component of PFM, including the management of revenues, public expenditures, public investments, public debt, state property and public procurement.

Under revenue management, the launch of the medium-term Revenue Mobilization Strategy 2014–18 and subsequent Revenue Mobilization

Strategy 2019–23 have significantly increased tax revenues in recent years. This is reflected in the ratio of the government's domestic revenue to GDP, which rose from 10.3 per cent in 2004 to 22.0 per cent in 2018. This increase is primarily attributed to reforms in GDT and GDCE, which raise most of the government's revenue.

The main feature of public expenditure management is to promote fiscal discipline, allocative efficiency and operational efficiency. The increase in revenue has provided the government with more flexibility in its spending. This is most evident in the increased spending on the public sector minimum wage, which was raised from KHR340,000 (US$85) in 2013 to more than KHR1 million (US$250) in 2018. Capital expenditure has also substantially increased, especially in the infrastructure, education and health sectors.

Public Investment Management (PIM), which generally refers to public infrastructures such as roads, airports, seaports, schools, and hospitals, is financed from the government state budget and external borrowings. The funding sources can vary depending on the types of public investment, leading to the problems of integrating and streamlining capital and current budgets. The adoption of the PIM system reform strategy 2019–25 paved the way for an integrated national system for managing public investment from all fund sources.

In terms of public debt management, the RGC has been successful at keeping the debt-to-GDP ratio well below the IMF's debt sustainability threshold (21.3 per cent of GDP at the end of 2019). Cambodia's Strategy on Public Debt Management 2019–23 set four guiding principles to loan policy: (1) ratio of credit to the scale of economy and budget, (2) concessional loan with low interest, (3) priority sectors with high growth and productivity, and (4) transparency, accountability, efficiency and effectiveness. The low debt-to-GDP ratio has provided the government with more confidence in its financial credibility.

NOTES
1. Special Drawing Rights (SDR) refers to an international type of monetary reserve currency created by the International Monetary Fund (IMF) in 1969 that operates as a supplement to the existing money reserves of member countries.
2. The Public Expenditure and Financial Accountability (PEFA) program provides

a framework for assessing and reporting on the strengths and weaknesses of a nation's PFM. It was founded by an international consortium that includes the World Bank and the European Union.
3. Refer to the Standards for the Professional Practice of Internal Auditing, Ministry of Economy and Finance, Cambodia.
4. Refer to Article 14 of the Law of Audit of the Kingdom of Cambodia.

CHAPTER FIVE

PFM System Assessment Tools

Many tools are available for assessing and monitoring public financial management systems, including:

- the Public Expenditure and Financial Accountability (PEFA) framework;
- the Open Budget Survey (OBS);
- the Public Investment Management Assessment (PIMA); and
- the Tax Administration Diagnostic Assessment Tool (TADAT).

These tools are used by external institutions to assess projects, institutions and programs to improve the management of PFM outputs and outcomes. They can also monitor and evaluate PFM reform efforts. The application of these tools can act as an external navigation system that helps the ship safely reach its destination.

This chapter discusses each of these PFM assessment tools in detail.

5.1 PUBLIC EXPENDITURE AND FINANCIAL ACCOUNTABILITY FRAMEWORK

The Public Expenditure and Financial Accountability (PEFA) framework is a program designed to provide snapshots of PFM performance at specific points in time that can be used in successive assessments and provide a summary of changes over time. It provides a framework for assessing and reporting on the strengths and weaknesses of PFM using quantitative indicators to measure performance. The PEFA framework includes a reporting mechanism that provides an overview of the PFM system and its performance. It can create a foundation for reform planning, dialogue on strategy and priorities, and progress monitoring.

PEFA is also a critical tool that can help governments achieve sustainable improvements in PFM practices by providing a means to measure and monitor performance using a set of indicators across a range of public financial management institutions, systems, and processes. The PEFA methodology draws on international standards and good practices for PFM, as identified by experienced practitioners.

PEFA offers a common basis for examining PFM performance across national and subnational governments. PEFA scores and reports allow all users of the information to gain a quick overview of the strengths and weaknesses of a country's PFM system. In addition to guidance for analysis and reporting, the PEFA Secretariat provides support, monitoring, and analysis of PEFA assessments. The PEFA Secretariat offers free advice on the use of PEFA as one of many sources of information for examining and improving PFM performance.

5.1.1 Scope and Coverage of the Framework

What Does PEFA Assess?

The purpose of a sound PFM system is to ensure that a government's policies are implemented as intended and achieve its objectives. An open and orderly PFM system is one of the enabling elements needed for desirable fiscal and budgetary outcomes, such as aggregate fiscal discipline, strategic allocation of resources, and efficient service delivery.

PEFA identifies seven pillars of performance in an open and orderly PFM system that are essential to achieving these objectives. The seven pillars define the key elements of a PFM system (see Figure 5.1):

1. *Budget reliability:* The government budget is realistic and is implemented as intended. This is measured by comparing actual revenues and expenditures with the original approved budget.
2. *Transparency of public finances:* Information on PFM is comprehensive, consistent and accessible to users. This is achieved through comprehensive budget classification and transparency of all government revenue and expenditure.

FIGURE 5.1
Interrelationship with the Seven Pillars of PEFA

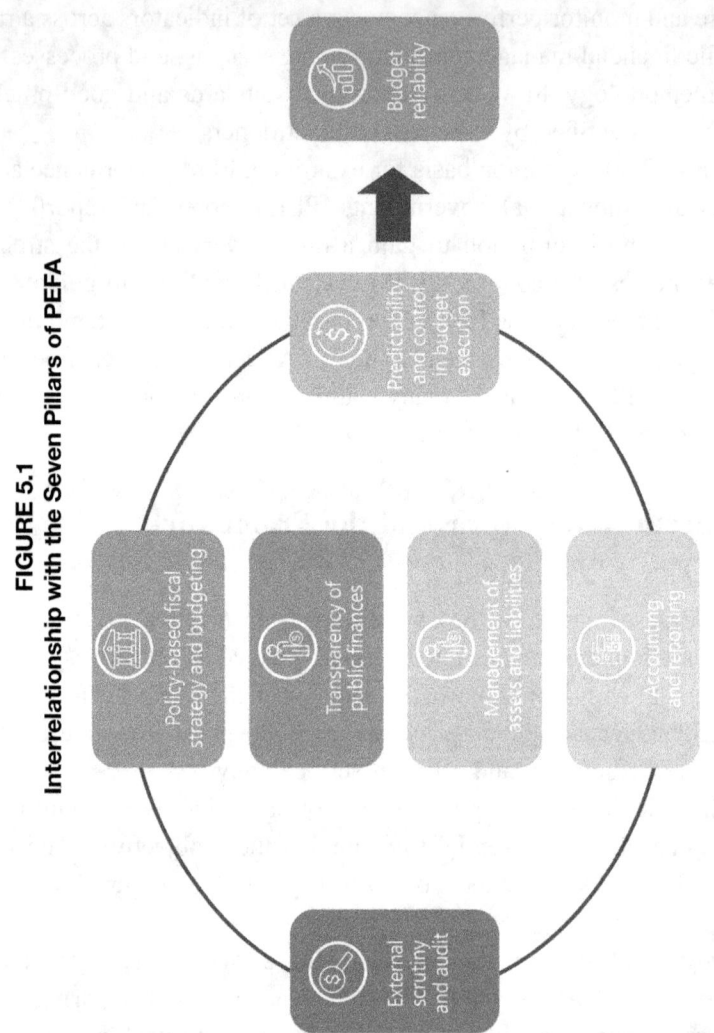

Source: PEFA 2016 Handbook (2018).

3. *Management of assets and liabilities:* Effective management of assets and liabilities ensures that public investments provide value for money, assets are recorded and managed, fiscal risks are identified, and debts and guarantees are prudently planned, approved and monitored.
4. *Policy-based fiscal strategy and budgeting:* The fiscal strategy and the budget are prepared with due regard to government fiscal policies, strategic plans and adequate macroeconomic and fiscal projections.
5. *Predictability and control in budget execution:* The budget is implemented within a system of effective standards, processes and internal controls, ensuring that resources are obtained and used as intended.
6. *Accounting and reporting:* Accurate and reliable records are maintained, and information is produced and disseminated at appropriate times to meet decision-making, management and reporting needs.
7. *External scrutiny and audit:* Public finances are independently reviewed and there is an external follow-up on the implementation of recommendations for improvement by the executive.

Within the seven broad areas marked by these pillars, PEFA defines thirty-one specific indicators that focus on key measurable aspects of the PFM system. PEFA uses the results of the individual indicator calculations, which are based on available evidence, to provide an integrated assessment of the PFM system against the seven pillars of PFM performance. It then assesses the likely impact of PFM performance levels on the three desired budgetary outcomes: aggregate fiscal discipline, strategic allocation of resources, and efficient service delivery.

What Institutions Does the PEFA Cover?

The core PEFA methodology was initially focused on central government, including related oversight and accountability institutions. However, PEFA has increasingly been used in the assessment of subnational government PFM performance. The scope of the category of "central government", as used in PEFA, is based on the classification structure developed by the International Monetary Fund (IMF) for Government Finance Statistics (GFS). The PEFA methodology refers to the GFS terminology where possible to provide a standard basis of reference, but this does not imply that PEFA is only relevant where GFS methodology is used. PEFA is adaptable to situations where other classifications and standards are used.

What Does the PEFA Not Include?

The PEFA indicators focus on the operational performance of key elements of the PFM system rather than on all the various inputs and capabilities that may enable the PFM system to reach a certain level of performance. The PEFA thus does not measure every factor affecting PFM performance, such as the legal framework or human resource capacities within the government. These are matters that should be considered.

PEFA also does not involve fiscal or expenditure policy analysis that would evaluate the sustainability of fiscal policy. It does not evaluate whether expenditures incurred through the budget ultimately reduce poverty or achieve other policy objectives or whether value for money is achieved in service delivery. PEFA focuses on assessing how the PFM system is an enabling factor for achieving such outcomes.

PEFA does not provide recommendations for reforms or assumptions about the potential impact of ongoing reforms on PFM performance. However, PEFA does acknowledge actions taken by governments to reform PFM systems by describing recent and ongoing measures. The PEFA report thus summarizes the government's reform agenda but does not evaluate it. Such considerations inform actions to be taken after the PEFA assessment and may form part of the dialogue between relevant stakeholders that contribute to the development of a new PFM improvement initiative.

5.1.2 The PEFA Performance Indicators

PEFA has thirty-one performance indicators across the broad array of PFM activities performed by governments. Table 5.1 shows the indicators are grouped under the seven pillars as the following:

Each pillar comprises a group of indicators that capture the performance of key systems, processes, and institutions of government. Each indicator includes one or more performance dimensions. Each dimension of the indicators measures performance against a four-point ordinal scale from A to D. Calibration of dimensions is based on the presence of important attributes relevant to different standards of performance. The highest score

TABLE 5.1
PEFA Pillars and Indicators

Pillars	Indicators
I. Budget reliability	1. Aggregate expenditure outturn 2. Expenditure composition outturn 3. Revenue outturn
II. Transparency of public financial data	4. Budget classification 5. Budget documentation 6. Central government operations outside financial reports 7. Transfers to subnational governments 8. Performance information for service delivery 9. Public access to fiscal information
III. Management of assets and liabilities	10. Fiscal risk reporting 11. Public investment management 12. Public asset management 13. Debt management
IV. Policy-based fiscal strategy and budgeting	14. Macroeconomic and fiscal forecasting 15. Fiscal strategy 16. Medium-term perspective in expenditure budgeting 17. Budget preparation process 18. Legislative scrutiny of budgets
V. Predictability and control in budget execution	19. Revenue administration 20. Accounting for revenue 21. Predictability of in-year resource allocation 22. Expenditure arrears 23. Payroll controls 24. Procurement 25. Internal controls on non-salary expenditure 26. Internal audit
VI. Accounting and reporting	27. Financial data integrity 28. In-year budget reports 29. Annual financial reports
VII. External scrutiny and audit	30. External audit 31. Legislative scrutiny of audit reports

Source: *PEFA 2016 Handbook* (2018).

is warranted for an individual dimension if the core PFM element meets an internationally recognized standard of good performance.

5.1.3 Public Expenditure and Financial Accountability for Subnational Level

PFM arrangements at the subnational level are likely to depend on structures determined by the central government, national legislation or national constitution. PFM arrangements can vary considerably by country reflecting differences in population and geographic size, governance, functions and administrative traditions.

Subnational PEFA assessments use the same indicators as the national government PEFA assessments with some adjustments. An additional indicator is included for assessing transfers and earmarked grants to subnational governments from higher-level governments. This indicator assesses the extent to which transfers to the subnational government from a higher-level government are consistent with original approved high-level budgets and are provided according to acceptable time frames.

5.1.4 Cambodia PEFA Assessment in 2015

PEFA assessments have been conducted three times in Cambodia—in 2010, 2015 and 2020.[1] A summary of findings was provided after the completion of each of the 2010 and 2015 assessments.

The 2015 PEFA Assessment's main objective was to provide an update of the 2010 PEFA report to take stock of achievements to date and to contribute to improving and focusing on Consolidate Action Plan 3, which was formulated in 2015. This repeat assessment became a basis for identifying and determining the possible effects of the previous reform programs and the ways forward. The assessment was focused on PFM systems' performance during FY2014 or the most recent period before that for which data was available.

The results of the assessment were an important reference for the government, development partners, and other stakeholders in identifying the major gaps or deficiencies of the PFM system as well as validating the effectiveness of past reforms. Analysis of these gaps or deficiencies then assisted the government in formulating future PFM reforms under CAP 3 and assisting the development partners in formulating the appropriate assistance to the government and as a reference for a similar assessment in the future.

The grades, A through D descending, for the performance indicators (PI) given to Cambodia's PFM for the two assessments are in Table 5.2. It is important to note that not all scores are fully comparable between the two assessment times, due to changes in how the indicators were measured. In addition, each indicator is comprised of several "dimensions" that in aggregate provide the overall grade for the performance indicator.

The PEFA assessment had the following findings:

Budget credibility (PI-1 to PI-4) has remained strong as regards budget outturns at the aggregate level for both domestic revenue and domestically financed expenditure (PI-1 and PI-3). Performance in this respect was already good in 2010 but has improved further. These results have not been affected by externally financed expenditure despite poor predictability of budget support while external project funding has generally met the budgeted amounts in aggregate.

On the other hand, budget credibility had deteriorated as regards the intended strategic allocation of resources to the main budget entities, despite already showing significant weaknesses in 2010 (PI-2). It is also a concern that expenditure arrears were high and that the systems to monitor arrears were incomplete so the overall level of arrears and its developments from year to year are not known (PI-4).

Comprehensiveness and transparency of the budget (PI-5 to PI-10) generally scored in the C to D range, except systems related to the central government's interaction with subnational administration which performs better. The comprehensiveness of the budget is still undermined by significant elements of government operations not being adequately reflected in the key fiscal reports of government—mainly as regards the operations of public administrative entities and externally funded projects (PI-7 scoring C in both years). The budget and accounts classification systems remain essentially at the basic level covering administrative and economic classification only, despite considerable efforts to add functional and program classification—as these new parts of the classification have yet to be fully developed and rolled out across budget entities (PI-5 scoring C in both years).

Meanwhile, slippage in performance had been found as regards budget transparency. Key information in the budget plan submitted to the legislature (and publicized after legislative approval) has been reduced (the score of PI-6 dropping from B in 2010 to C in 2015) and the access of the public at large to key fiscal information has also dropped (the score of PI-10 reduced from C in 2010 to D 2015) due to long delays in making the requisite information available, despite the reports being produced timely for internal use.

Transparency and predictability in the intergovernmental relations between the central government and Communes/*Sangkats* remain high as transfers to communes and *Sangkats* are rules-based and the indicative transfer estimates are provided well on time and are reliable. The oversight of commune's/*Sangkat's* fiscal operations ensures that the central government does not face fiscal risks from those entities. Yet, the central government is unable to report strategic allocation to sectors or programs at the aggregate level of general government as classification systems are different at central government and subnational administrative levels and neither one includes comprehensive functional or sector classification. Monitoring of fiscal risk from commercial public enterprises has also remained weak as no overview of fiscal risks is prepared and reported, an issue worsened by the lack of ceilings for the issue of guarantees by the government.

Policy-based budgeting (PI-11 to PI-12) showed strong performance in the process of preparing the annual budget, a comprehensive process, organized in several distinct stages with appropriate involvement of both the top political level and the individual line ministries and completed on time every year. This good performance has been maintained since 2010 (PI-11 scoring A in both years). However, the medium-term aspects of policy-based budgeting are performing less well and little progress has been noted since 2010. This makes it difficult to sustain support for policy priorities in the medium to long term. Sector strategies with full costing in line with fiscal aggregates are still the exception, and budgeting of recurrent and capital project expenditures remain separate processes with weak links. While a medium-term budget framework is prepared annually, the links between the estimates from one year to the next are weak. An exception is the analysis of debt sustainability, which has remained strong

TABLE 5.2
Change in Performance Between 2010 and 2015

	PFM Performance Indicators	2010	2015	Scores Comparable	Performance Change
PI-1	Aggregate expenditure out-turn compared to original approved budget	B	A	No	←
PI-2	Composition of expenditure out-turn compared to original approved budget	D	D+	No	→
PI-3	Aggregate revenue out-turn compared to original approved budget	A	A	No	←
PI-4	Stock and monitoring of expenditure payment arrears	C+	D+	No	?
PI-5	Classification of the budget	C	C	Yes	No change
PI-6	Comprehensiveness of information included in budget documentation	B	C	Yes	→
PI-7	Extent of unreported government operations	C	C	Yes	No change
PI-8	Transparency of inter-governmental fiscal relations	C+	B	No	No change
PI-9	Oversight of aggregate fiscal risk from other public sector entities	C+	C+	Yes	No change
PI-10	Public access to key fiscal information	C	D	No	→
PI-11	Orderliness and participation in the annual budget process	A	A	Yes	No change
PI-12	Multi-year perspective in fiscal planning, expenditure policy and budgeting	B	C+	Yes	No change
PI-13	Transparency of taxpayer obligations and liabilities	B	C+	No	No change
PI-14	Effectiveness of measures for taxpayer registration and tax assessment	C	D+	No	No change

PI-15	Effectiveness in collection of tax payments	D+	D+	Yes	No change
PI-16	Predictability in the availability of funds for commitment of expenditures	C+	C+	Yes	←
PI-17	Recording and management of cash balances, debt and guarantees	C+	C+	Yes	No change
PI-18	Effectiveness of payroll controls	D+	D+	Yes	No change
PI-19	Competition, value for money and controls in procurement	C	D+	No	?
PI-20	Effectiveness of internal controls for non-salary expenditure	C	C	No	No change
PI-21	Effectiveness of internal audit	D+	C	Yes	←
PI-22	Timeliness and regularity of accounts reconciliation	C	C	Yes	No change
PI-23	Availability of information on resources received by service delivery units	C	D	No	No change
PI-24	Quality and timeliness of in-year budget reports	C+	C	Yes	←
PI-25	Quality and timeliness of annual financial statements	D+	D+	Yes	←
PI-26	Scope, nature and follow-up of external audit	D+	NR	Partial	←
PI-27	Legislative scrutiny of the annual budget law	NU	C+	NA	?
PI-28	Legislative scrutiny of external audit reports	NU	B	NA	?
D-1	Predictability of Direct Budget Support	C	D	No	→
D-2	Financial info provided by donors on project/program aid	D	D+	Yes	←
D-3	Proportion of aid that is managed by use of national procedures	D	D	Yes	←

Source: Report of the Evaluation on the Public Financial Management System of Cambodia (2015).

and where the government has enhanced its internal capacity to undertake the analysis annually.

Predictability and control in budget execution (PI-13 to PI-21): All of the nine indicators in this area score low, i.e., in the C to D range, although particular dimensions of many of the indicators perform better. On the side of revenue administration, little appears to have changed since 2010. The law on taxation has several gaps, providing the administration with extensive discretion, and the provision for an independent appeals tribunal has not been implemented. Efforts are being made to give taxpayers access to relevant information, but limited human and financial capacity mean that the information is not always comprehensive and up to date (PI-13). Ensuring compliance with tax registration and filing is made difficult by a lack of proactive approaches to capturing all businesses tax, inadequate levels and enforcement of penalties for non-compliance, by an approach to taxpayer audits that are not sufficiently risk-based (PI-14).

Tax collection could also be improved significantly. Tax arrears remain high despite slight improvements in collection rates, and monitoring is hampered because full reconciliation of collections with tax assessments and arrears happens only on an annual basis. However, the revenue float remains low as collections are transferred to the national treasury with little delay (PI-15).

Cash flow forecasting, a dimension of PI-16, is performing well and has improved in recent years, but in-year reallocations are frequent and significant and can lead to outturns quite different from the budgeted allocations. Debt management systems are fair but of minor importance due to the relatively low level of government debt. Consolidation of cash balances (a dimension of PI-17) performs well and has not changed since 2010.

Monitoring of compliance with procurement regulations is hampered by a lack of data (PI-19). In the area of staff salaries (PI-18), personnel and payroll data are not directly linked, and comprehensive payroll audits are not conducted. Moreover, payroll changes are often delayed and result in payment arrears. Internal controls of non-salary expenditures are not comprehensive and audit reports indicate frequent non-compliance with the rules (PI-20). The internal audit function is still in its infancy, but a positive development is more attention to systemic issues by the internal audit units, rather than transaction-based audits (PI-21).

Accounting, recording and reporting: The four performance indicators in this area (PI-22 to PI-25) generally scored low, in the range of C to D, but positive developments are noted for several of the indicator's dimensions. Bank reconciliations continue to be done comprehensively and on time, and the timeliness of preparing the in-year budget execution reports has improved. Lastly, the preparation of annual financial statements has seen distinct improvements in both timeliness and disclosure of accounting standards, but still rates low for the overall performance indicator.

External scrutiny and audit: Institutional coverage of external audit and adherence to international audit standards remain low, but timeliness in a completed audit of the annual financial statements improved significantly.

The oversight functions of the national legislature generally performed well, with B scores in many of the dimensions of PI-27 and PI-28. However, the involvement of the legislature in the budget process is limited due to the review of the budget plan at a stage where all details have already been prepared by the government, and because of the extensive powers of the MEF to reallocate funds without prior legislative approval. It is not possible to judge change since 2010 as the two indicators of legislative oversight were not assessed in 2010.

Donor practices: Indicators on donor practices continued to score low with all three indicators scoring in the D range. The predictability of budget support has deteriorated, but the importance of budget support has also declined and so the impact of this deterioration is very modest. Improvements have been made in reporting on project support both for budgeting purposes and *ex-post* reporting on actual disbursements. However, *ex-post* reporting is still too fragmented and late to allow full coverage in budget execution reports. Use of country systems remains low (D-3 scoring D in both years) but hides a significant improvement from a level of 12–15 per cent in 2010 to now about 25 per cent of all external assistance—even if this is insufficient to increase the score.

5.1.5 Summary of Performance Changes Since 2010

Table 5.2 compares the scores of the performance indicators of the 2015 PEFA assessment with the scores from the 2010 PEFA report. The fifth column indicates whether it is meaningful to directly compare the scores of the two assessments. Comparisons could not be made for 15 of the 31 indicators. The reasons for non-comparability are: (a) that the indicator structure and/or scoring criteria for three indicators were changed by the PEFA Program in 2011 (PI-2, PI-3 and PI-19), or (b) that the 2010 scores were not established on the same basis as the current scores due to either lack of data in 2010 or a different interpretation of the data requirements and their implications for the scores. Comparisons were made for the remaining sixteen indicators. Results for the dimensions of the performance indicators are not shown.

Performance improvement (upward arrow) is indicated for two of the sixteen indicators, whereas performance slippage (downward arrow) is found for three indicators. The remaining eleven performance indicators do not show any significant change in either direction.

5.2 OPEN BUDGET SURVEY

The Open Budget Survey (OBS) is a comprehensive survey and analysis that evaluates whether governments give their citizens access to budget information and opportunities to participate in the budget process at the national level. The survey also assesses the capacity and independence of formal oversight institutions.

Using two-year intervals, the International Budget Partnership (IBP), works with civil society partners in 117 countries, including Cambodia, to conduct the OBS as of 2019. Surveys have been completed in 2006, 2008, 2010, 2012, 2015, 2017 and 2019. The IBP, established in 1997, is an international non-governmental organization focused on ensuring that government budget systems are more transparent and accountable to the public and thereby more responsive to the needs of the poor.

5.2.1 Methodology of Open Budget Survey

OBS assesses three components of a budget accountability system: (1) public availability of budget information; (2) opportunities for citizens to participate in the budget process; and (3) the role and effectiveness of formal oversight institutions, including the legislature and the national audit office (referred to here as the "supreme audit institution"). The majority of the survey questions assess what occurs in practice rather than what is required by law.

The questions included in the OBS are based on generally accepted good practices for public financial management. For example, the survey assesses the public availability of budget information by considering the timely release and contents of eight key budget documents that all countries might issue at different points in the budget process. Many of these criteria are drawn from those developed by multilateral organizations, such as the International Monetary Fund's (IMF) Code of Good Practices on Fiscal Transparency, the Public Expenditure and Finance Accountability Initiative, the Organization for Economic Co-operation and Development's (OECD) Best Practices for Fiscal Transparency, and the International Organization of Supreme Audit Institutions' Lima Declaration of Guidelines on Auditing Precepts. Similarly, the criteria used to assess opportunities for citizens to participate in the budget process are based on the Global Initiative for Fiscal Transparency's Principles for Public Participation in Fiscal Policy.

5.2.2 Structure of the Open Budget Survey

The OBS is divided into five sections with around 150 questions organized into five sections:

- Public Availability of Key Budget Documents;
- The Comprehensiveness of the Executive's Budget Proposal;
- The Comprehensiveness of Other Key Budget Documents;
- Role and Effectiveness of the Oversight Institutions; and
- Public Engagement in the Budget Process.

The questions asked include inquiries about the contents of key budget reports that all governments are expected to publish, legislatures and supreme audit institutions' roles and powers, public engagement opportunities in budgeting, and the specifics of expenditures, revenues, and debt.

5.2.3 The Importance of Budget Transparency and Accountability

Over the past decade, there has been growing evidence that the best way to improve the management of public finances is through transparent budget systems, open to citizens' engagement and scrutiny, and robust oversight institutions and mechanisms. In particular, several research studies have demonstrated how open budgeting practices can have a positive impact on many desirable outcomes.

A comprehensive review of existing evidence on the impacts of fiscal openness found that greater fiscal transparency brings about several beneficial results, including lower government borrowing costs due to macro-fiscal disclosure, lower corruption costs, and greater electoral accountability of politicians (de Renzio and Wehner 2017).[2]

Research has provided evidence that transparency can support macroeconomic stability. For example, the IMF found that higher levels of fiscal transparency can lead to greater fiscal credibility and performance, as well as cheaper international credit (IMF 2012).[3] Another study by Sarr (2015) found that transparent countries are more likely to have budgets that are credible and reliable, thereby supporting the effective delivery of public services and macroeconomic stability.[4] A survey conducted by the IBP indicates that investors consider the absence of fiscal information to be a signal of undisclosed fiscal weakness and that decisions on whether and how much to invest in a country are often influenced by its level of budget transparency.[5]

Transparency and public participation in budgeting can create more efficient resource allocation and improvements in service delivery outcomes. Governments (municipalities) that adopt participatory practices, such as public policy councils and participatory budgeting, collect significantly more local taxes. The result shows that—regardless of government systems and levels of development and culture—citizens are more committed to tax compliance when they can voice their preferences about government spending and learn about government oversight of public resources (Touchton, Wampler, and Peixoto 2019; Sjoberg et al. 2019).[6]

Other research has demonstrated that: the adoption of participatory budgeting is associated with changes in resource allocation, especially increases in health and education programs (Touchton and Wampler 2014);[7] increased transparency has often contributed to increased and improved budget allocations towards development goals;[8] and a civil society coalition used its access to information on health budgets to petition a case in court to increase government spending on HIV/AIDS treatments by US$6 billion, providing lifesaving medicines to 1.6 million people (Overy 2011).[9]

5.2.4 Cambodian Open Budget Survey in 2019

According to the open budget survey in 2019, Cambodia ranked 86 among 117 countries for public availability of budget information. In terms of score, as shown in Figure 5.2, Cambodia's score in public availability of budget information has improved significantly during the last ten years, from only 11 in 2008 to 32 points in 2019. Despite this improvement, this score is still below the global average score of 45. In general, a score of 61 is considered the minimum threshold to foster an informed public debate on budgets.

Cambodia has increased the availability of budget information by publishing a year-end report and part of the executive's budget. Cambodia publishes eight key budget documents but scores only 32 on the OBS 2019 budget transparency assessment because many documents are missing essential details and are therefore of limited use to anyone trying to identify and monitor approved public spending. The assessment report recommends Cambodia prioritize some actions to improve budget transparency, including (1) publishing the complete Executive's Budget Proposal, including all supporting documents, online before the National Assembly approves the

FIGURE 5.2
Trend in Scoring of Public Availability of Budget Information

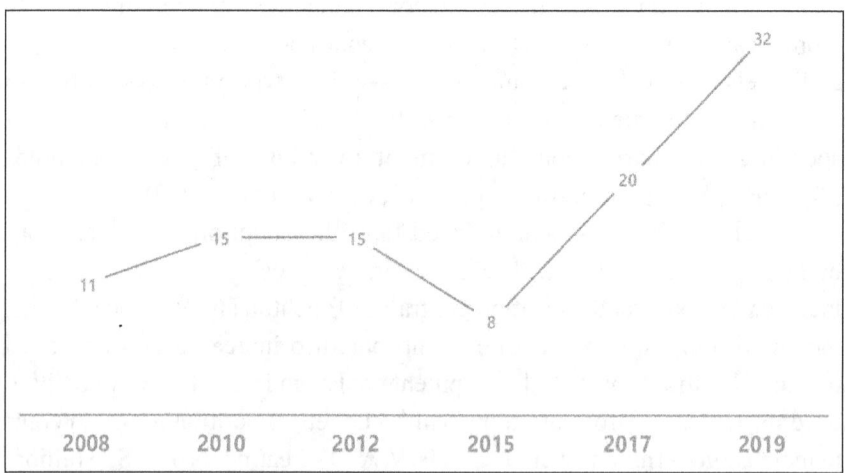

Source: Author's illustration.

budget; (2) including debt and performance information in the year-end report; (3) seeking public input on the content of the Citizens Budget; and (4) strengthening the follow-up on the Audit Report by having the executive issue a report tracking steps taken to respond to audit findings.

Regarding public participation, the report recommends that the MEF establish public consultations during budget implementation, pilot mechanisms to engage the public during budget formulation, and regular forums or mechanisms for the public to contribute to budget monitoring. The report also recommends actively engaging with vulnerable and underrepresented communities, either directly or through civil society organizations representing them.

The legislature and the supreme audit institution in Cambodia, together, provide limited oversight during the budget process, with a composite OBS oversight score of 50 (out of 100). Cambodia's Parliament provides limited oversight during the planning and execution stage of the budget cycle. To improve this oversight, the legislature should debate budget policy before the Executive's Budget Proposal is tabled and approve recommendations for the upcoming budget. Legislative committees should examine the Executive's budget proposal and the annual Audit Report and publish reports with their analysis online. In addition, a committee should examine the in-year budget implementation and publish reports online with their findings. In general, the legislature should be consulted before the executive spends any unanticipated revenue or reduces spending due to revenue shortfalls.

5.3 PUBLIC INVESTMENT MANAGEMENT ASSESSMENT

The Public Investment Management Assessment (PIMA) is a comprehensive tool created by the IMF to assess infrastructure governance for countries at all levels of economic development. To make its assessments, PIMA examines procedures, tools, decision-making, and monitoring processes used by the governments to provide infrastructure assets and services to the citizen. The PIMA framework will help identify reform priorities and classify the practical actions for implementation. The tool focuses on two main aspects of public investment management: institutional design (what is on paper) and effectiveness (actual implementation). There are fifteen main indicators in the framework plus three cross-cutting enabling factors for supporting infrastructure governance, as shown in Figure 5.3.

PIMA is a new tool introduced in 2015 to help IMF member countries strengthen their infrastructure governance practices. Cambodia was in the first set of test countries that were assessed, thus contributing to the development of the PIMA tool. There are nearly sixty countries around the world, which have been assessed and the results provide a broad picture of infrastructure management systems for the assessed countries, from investment planning and medium-term budget allocation to project implementation. Moreover, the assessed countries then know the gaps in their PIM system and can refocus reform priorities. The findings and recommendations of PIMA are tailored to each country's needs and capacities and summarized in a sequenced and prioritized reform action plan. The PIMA reports also help countries mobilize the resources to support the PIM system's reform action plan, especially with development partners.

5.3.1 Cambodia PIMA in 2019

Cambodia has made a significant effort to increase public investment over the past few decades, but it still needs a more systematically developed infrastructure for the whole country. The assessment result shows that Cambodia is still one of the lowest capital stock-per-capita nations in the region, which leaves room for improvement in the efficiency of public investment management. As shown in Figure 5.4, the institutional strength of PIM in Cambodia (on paper) is much better than the actual effectiveness (in practice). One of the biggest challenges that PIMA identified is the management process for projects funded by domestic finance, particularly since there is no list of the projects in the budget document during the budget approval process.

There are six main priority recommendations that the PIMA report suggests for the government to improve its infrastructure governance:

1. Implement a full-fledged medium-term fiscal framework to provide multi-year guidance for budget preparation and assessment of fiscal risks (including public-private partnerships or PPPs).

FIGURE 5.3
PIMA Framework

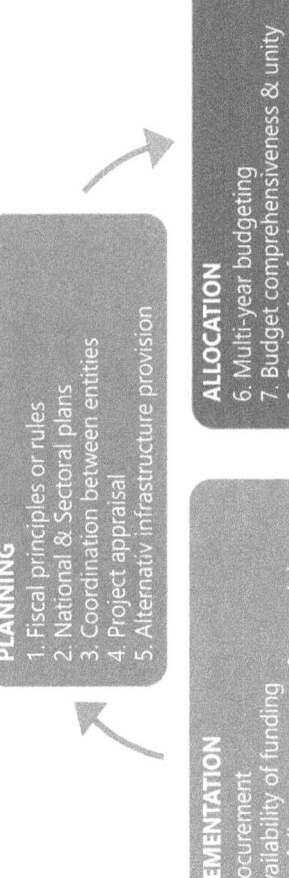

PLANNING
1. Fiscal principles or rules
2. National & Sectoral plans
3. Coordination between entities
4. Project appraisal
5. Alternativ infrastructure provision

ALLOCATION
6. Multi-year budgeting
7. Budget comprehensiveness & unity
8. Budgeting for investment
9. Maintenance funding
10. Project selection

IMPLEMENTATION
11. Procurement
12. Availability of funding
13. Portfolio management & oversight
14. Management of project implementation
15. Monitoring of public assets

CROSS CUTTING ENABLING FACTORS

IT Systems | Legal and institutional frameworks | Staff Capacity

Source: Public Investment Management Assessment (PIMA) (2019).

PFM System Assessment Tools • 119

FIGURE 5.4
Institutional Strength and Effectiveness of PIM Institutions in Cambodia

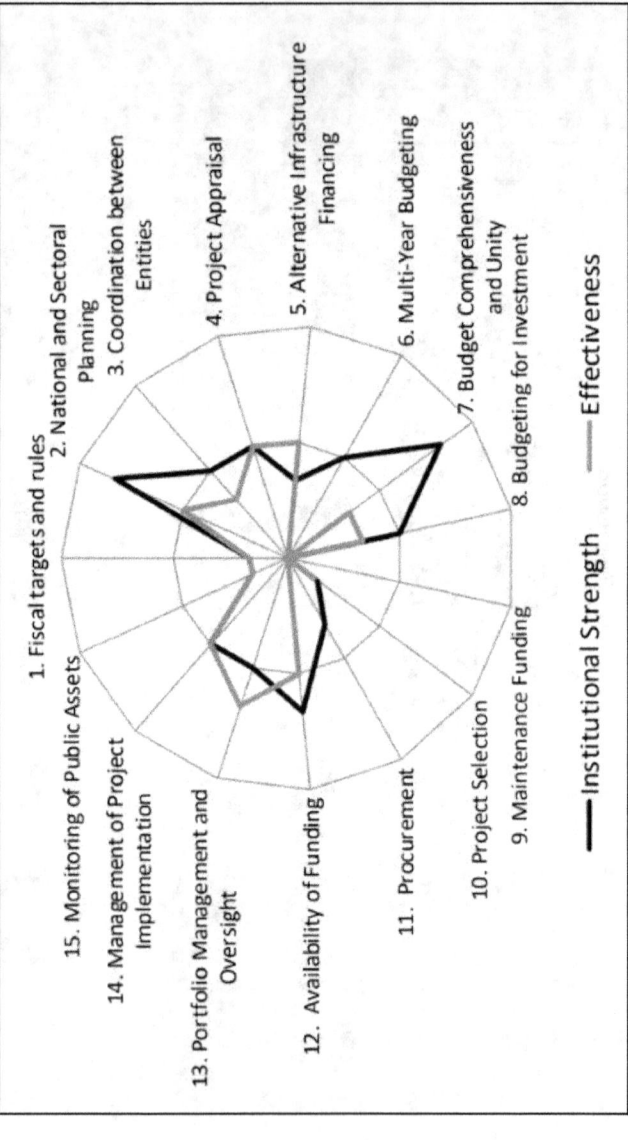

Source: Cambodia Public Investment Management Assessment (PIMA) (2019).

2. Identify individual projects during budget preparation to improve the coordination of capital and recurrent budgets and include the list in the budget documents.
3. Provide a comprehensive picture of investment projects in the budget documentation, regardless of their financing source (including externally funded projects and PPPs).
4. Build in-house capacity for project preparation and review to provide quality assurance before implementing a project.
5. Develop capacity and tools to centrally monitor project delays and cost overruns, using multiyear budget information.
6. Strengthen in-year monitoring of individual domestically financed projects by line ministries.

5.4 TAX ADMINISTRATION DIAGNOSTIC ASSESSMENT TOOL

The Tax Administration Diagnostic Assessment Tool (TADAT) is designed to provide an objective assessment of the health of key components of a country's system of tax administration. Cambodia had a TADAT assessment in 2020; the results are expected shortly.

The TADAT framework is focused on nine key performance outcome areas (POAs) that cover most tax administration functions, processes and institutions. The assessment of these performance outcome areas is based on 32 high-level indicators built on 1 to 4 dimensions that add up to 55 measurement dimensions, making TADAT a comprehensive but administrable diagnostic tool.

TADAT assessments are particularly helpful in:

- identifying the relative strengths and weaknesses of tax administration systems, processes and institutions;
- facilitating a shared view on the condition of the system administration among all stakeholders (e.g., country authorities, international organizations, donor countries and technical assistance providers);
- selling the reform agenda, including reform objectives, priorities, initiatives, and implementation sequencing;
- facilitating management and coordination of external support for reforms and achieving faster and more efficient implementation; and

- monitoring and evaluating reform progress by way of subsequent repeat assessments.

5.4.1 Scope and Coverage of the Framework

TADAT is a global tool that can be used by any country to assess the relative strengths and weaknesses of its tax administration system. TADAT assessments focus on the administration of the major direct and indirect taxes critical to central government revenues. Accordingly, TADAT assessments are based on administration-specific taxes, which collectively are referred to as "core taxes", which serve as proxies for all national taxes. TADAT is not designed to assess the administration of special tax regimes, such as those applying in the natural resource sector. Nor does TADAT assess customs administration.[10] TADAT provides an assessment within the country's existing revenue policy framework, with evaluations highlighting performance issues that may be best dealt with by a mix of administrative and policy responses.

5.4.2 Emerging Lessons for the TADAT Framework

The TADAT method has found that the outcomes approach is viable and some countries (including those not assessed) are using the TADAT framework for internal benchmarking, particularly how far away are their systems of tax administration from the highest maturity level or the frontier tax administrations. However, a meaningful assessment requires the active involvement of the country's tax administration and related agency staff in all phases of the assessment.

Donors, development partners and TA providers, in general, can reinforce each other using TADAT results as a baseline. TADAT helps countries develop ownership and take the lead in managing the reform effort as well as embedding the TADAT methodology into their regular performance monitoring, reporting and accountability frameworks.

5.5 SUMMARY

PEFA framework is designed to provide a snapshot of PFM performance at specific points in time. It assesses and reports the PFM strengths and weaknesses, using quantitative indicators to measure performance. This framework covers seven pillars, including budget credibility; transparency of public financial management; management of assets and liabilities; policy-based fiscal strategy and budgeting; predictability and control in budget execution; accounting and reporting; and external scrutiny and audit. According to its website, PEFA's performance measurement framework has been applied over 220 times in more than 125 countries. Cambodia has used it three times, in 2010, 2015, and most recently in 2020.

OBS is the world's only independent comparable measure of budget transparency, participation and oversight. It assesses these three components of the budget accountability system. The first component reflects the public availability of budget information; the second is about opportunities for citizens to participate in the budget process; and the third describes the role and effectiveness of formal oversight institutions, including the legislature and the national audit office. Cambodia had a good experience using OBS which shows an upward trend of scoring in budget transparency, from 11 points in 2008 to 32 points in 2019.

The PIMA framework is used to assess infrastructure governance for countries at all levels of economic development and helps to identify reform priorities and classify the practical actions for implementation. The tool focuses on two main aspects of public investment management: institutional design and effectiveness. Cambodia has made a great effort to increase public investment over the past decades. The PIMA framework has shown that Cambodia is still one of the lowest capital stock-per-capita in the region, which leaves room for improvement in public investment management efficiency.

TADAT aims to provide a standardized means of assessing the health of key components of a country's tax administration system. The assessment focuses on the administration of major direct and indirect taxes critical to central/federal government revenues. It is based on the administration of specific taxes, which collectively are referred to as "core taxes", serving as the proxies for all national taxes. Cambodia is in the first process of a TADAT assessment, and the results were produced in 2021.

NOTES
1. This book only discusses the 2015 assessment result and its comparison to the 2010 assessment. Cambodia also uses the Subnational PEFA framework to assess the Phnom Penh Capital government.
2. Paolo de Renzio and Joachim Wehner, "The Impacts of Fiscal Openness", *World Bank Research Observer* 32 no. 2 (2017): 185–210.
3. International Monetary Fund, "Fiscal Transparency, Accountability, and Risk" (Washington, DC: IMF, 2012), http://www.imf.org/external/np/pp/eng/2012/080712.pdf
4. Babacar Sarr, "Credibility and Reliability of Government Budgets: Does Fiscal Transparency Matter?", International Budget Partnership, Working Paper No. 5. Washington, DC (2015), http://www.internationalbudget.org/publications/credibility-and-reliability-of-government-budgets-does-fiscal-transparency-matter/
5. In December 2014, the International Budget Partnership in collaboration with the Emerging Markets Investor Alliance conducted a survey of ten of the Alliance's member analysts from different investment houses to better understand the private sector's interest in fiscal transparency.
6. Michael Touchton, Brian Wampler, and Tiago Peixoto, "Of Governance and Revenue Participatory Institutions and Tax Compliance in Brazil", World Bank Group Policy Research Working Paper 8797 (2019), https://openknowledge.worldbank.org/bitstream/handle/10986/31492/WPS8797.pdf; Fredrik Matias Sjoberg, Jonathan Mellon, Tiago Carneiro Peixoto, Johannes Zacharias Hemker, and Lily Lee Tsai, "Voice and Punishment: A Global Survey Experiment on Tax Morale", World Bank Group Policy Research Working Paper 8855 (2019).
7. Michael Touchton, and Brian Wampler, "Improving Social Well-Being through New Democratic Institutions", *Comparative Political Studies* 47, no. 10 (2014): 1442–69.
8. International Budget Partnership, "From Numbers to Nurses: Why Budget Transparency, Expenditure Monitoring, and Accountability Are Vital to the Post-2015 Framework", *Budget Brief*, October 2014, https://www.internationalbudget.org/wp-content/uploads/Budget-Brief-From-Numbers-to-Nurses.pdf
9. Neil Overy, "In the Face of Crisis: The Treatment Action Campaign Fights Government Inertia with Budget Advocacy and Litigation", *International Budget Partnership*, Case Study Series No. 7, August 2011, https://www.internationalbudget.org/publications/in-the-face-of-crisis-the-treatment-action-campaign-fights-government-inertia-with-budget-advocacy-and-litigation/
10. The World Customs Organization has also developed and actively promotes a diagnostic process for customs reform and modernization.

CHAPTER SIX

Case Study

Public financial management reform is the backbone of all reforms in the Cambodian government. To achieve policy objectives at minimal costs, the government budget must be credible, and its expenditure be efficient, at both the national and subnational levels of government. This section describes the PFM reforms by selected ministries: the Ministry of Education, Youth, and Sport (MOEYS) and the Ministry of Rural Development (MRD). It also introduces reform of the PFM system at the subnational administration level.

The four largest spending ministries in Cambodia are MOEYS, the Ministry of National Defence (MOD), the Ministry of Interior (MOI) and the Ministry of Health (MOH), accounting for 60 per cent of the total government spending. Individually, their shares of the budget in 2020 were approximately 21 per cent, 17 per cent, 13 per cent, and 11 per cent, respectively. MOEYS was selected for case studies as they are big spenders and more representative of the majority of administrative structures of the government while MRD was also selected as it more directly impacts the locals. MOI and MOD have special characteristics that separate them from mainstream line ministries, given that they are also involved in the armed forces and police spending.

6.1 PFMRP AND IMPACT ON MOEYS

MOEYS was established in 1996 with a mission to lead and develop the educational sector and programs for youth and sports. MOEYS is the highest-spending ministry, compared to others in the Cambodian government, having a budget of 21 per cent of the government's total budget in 2020. Of this budget, 81 per cent was allocated to the salaries of teachers and staff. In the 1990s and early 2000s, when the government experienced budget shortages, MOEYS was more affected than others. Therefore, PRMRP Platform 1, which addressed this budget shortage, had a significant stabilizing effect on this ministry and the country's education sector as a whole.

Management Support and Acceptance within MOEYS

The Minister of Education, Youth and Sport is the Chair of MOEYS's PFMRP working group and is a champion of PFMRP as a whole. The director of MOEYS' Department of Finance and its deputy directors are also the drivers of the Ministry's reforms and have promoted clear and time-bounded action plans for reform.

The Education Strategic Plan (ESP) 2019–23 included a set of policy objectives related to PFMRP which include strengthening financial management processes for effective budget implementation and directly linking financial accountability with performance accountability. Senior staff at MOEYS acknowledged the importance of PFMRP with the belief that it would eventually provide tangible benefits to the ministry and improve the quality of education in the country. MOEYS has actively raised PFMRP among its employees both at the national and provincial levels by promoting the PFMRP agenda and encouraging employees' participation in the reforms.

Support from the Ministry of Economy and Finance

The MOEYS PFMRP Secretariat interacts with MEF every quarterly, particularly through the Ministerial Action Plan (MAP) quarterly progress meetings. In the meetings, MOEYS requested the adjustment of coordination and instruction from MEF. Specifically, during one of the PFMRP Technical Working Group (TWG) meetings, MOEYS and the development partners discussed and requested that MEF representatives amend their reporting of the progress of PFMRP about the MAP, which is based on the MEF Consolidated Action Plan (CAP), to include not only activities completed but also immediate results or outcomes. In other words, the report needs to help of the development partners' assistance. However, most of the IAD staff members are teachers and have limited audit qualifications and experience. The IAD Director reports to the Minister of Education, Youth and Sport.

6.2 PFMRP AND IMPACT ON THE MINISTRY OF RURAL DEVELOPMENT

The Ministry of Rural Development (MRD) was newly established after the 1993 Cambodian general election, with a vision to create long-term sustainable development in all rural areas by encouraging self-sufficiency. MRD's mission is to encourage and assist rural communities to participate more directly in improving farm production, rural-based industries and marketing of their products. It is generally understood that rural development would make a significant contribution to poverty reduction and promote the economic resilience of the people. MRD also has the responsibility to improve the quality of life for people in rural areas by encouraging and facilitating economic self-sufficiency and active social awareness, rather than relying on the central government or aid agencies to help.

Management Support and Acceptance within MRD

PFMRP has enjoyed strong support and acceptance from the leadership level of MRD. Senior staff members at the ministry's Department of Planning and International Cooperation (DPIC) and DoF welcome PFMRP and believe it will eventually provide tangible benefits to the ministry and rural development at large. MRD actively promotes the PFMRP agenda among its officials and staff members at the national and provincial levels.

MRD's Budget Strategic Plan (BSP) 2020–22 aims to guide how to develop programs for rural development to support the RGC National Strategic Development Plan 2019–23 and Cambodian Sustainable Development Goals 2030. One of the most important objectives of MRD's BSP is to continue to participate in the PFMRP in Stage 3 and Stage 4.

Support from the Ministry of Economy and Finance

MRD's DPIC and DoF interact with MEF every quarter, particularly at the MAP and CAP quarterly progress meetings. CAP and MAP systems have been working well at MRD, but going forward, improvement is needed to formulate annual results indicators and cumulative results indicators.

Capacity Issues

MRD took part in two capacity-building projects between 2009 and 2015, supported by the ADB, that aimed to facilitate its implementation of PFMRP. In 2009, when MRD first participated in PFMRP, many officials in the ministries appeared to understand the program well. With its participation in this capacity-building program, MRD became a champion for the reforms. Recently, MRD officials also received training from MEF on the Financial Management Information System (FMIS).

Recognizing the importance of human resource development, MRD introduced a policy to increase the capacity of its civil servants at national and provincial levels that will contribute to the implementation of the Public Administrative Reform Program, Public Financial Management Reform, Decentralization and De-concentration reform, and other reforms, to make the ministry more effective.

Budget Creditability

As a pilot ministry, MRD has been producing the BSP and introducing PB since the beginning of the PFMRP. Staff members have been extensively trained and have gained the necessary skills in formulating BSP and PB.

The BSP formulation is fully compliant with the "Circular on the Development of budget strategic plan 2020–2022". BSP 2020–22 is also well in line with the Rectangular Strategy, the National Strategic Development Plan, the Cambodian Sustainable Development Goals 2030, MRD's five-year Strategic Framework 2019–23, and various national action plans, such as the National Action Plan for the Improvement of Water Supply, Health and Rural Sanitation Phase 2, 2019–23 and the National Policy on Indigenous Peoples' Development. The plan also provides a good summary of the resources required from the government budget and development partners for implementation.

MRD has now identified important strengths in the budget preparation process and improved in-year budget predictability in coordination with MEF. MRD has also successfully implemented all the objectives of

Platform 1: Budget Credibility to maintain and strengthen the credibility of its budget. Although budget credibility has suffered due to the establishment of new budget entities that did not meet the intended strategic allocation of resources to the main budget entities, MRD has now fully adopted the budget entity system and is performing at the PEFA level of +/− 5 per cent budget execution.

Financial Accountability

Financial accountability within MRD is good at the operational level. The high level of spending on capital projects is in line with the nature of the ministry's work. MRD often has access to additional funding from RGC's reserves for maintenance, capital expenditure and climate disaster management in rural communities.

Capital expense and investment use the mechanism of the inter-ministry committee to prioritize projects. Investment needs are identified at the lowest levels possible—in communes and *Sangkats*—and are prioritized for discussion with MEF's Department of Investment. When the number of projects is reduced as a result of negotiations and reviews of economic and financial viability thresholds, they are prioritized and submitted to the inter-ministry committee.

MRD prepares the Public Investment Program (PIP) annually and submits it to the Ministry of Planning. This PIP is eventually shared with MEF and the Council for the Development of Cambodia (CDC). MRD negotiates directly with multilateral aid donors while CDC consults with bilateral aid agencies to finance any funding gaps from the national capital investment budget.

Stage 2 of the PFM reform program is defined as "Effective Financial Accountability", and is being achieved through effective budget reporting by the managers of subministerial budget entities, to whom budget accountability and decision-making have been delegated. MRD's Internal Audit Department assists and reports on this accountability.[1]

Internal Audit

The Internal Audit Department (IAD) is still in the process of developing capacity with assistance from development partners, particularly the ADB.

This capacity development program includes on-the-job training, workshops and seminars. Training is also conducted on manual preparation, drafting procedures and reporting formats, report preparation, field audits and compliance with standard operating procedures.

MRD's IAD is now fully staffed and operational. A master training strategy for all MRD internal audit staff members was developed in 2015 and fully delivered. All internal audit staff members have been trained on audit techniques under ADB support. Training includes coaching clinics, information-based training at the Economic and Finance Institute (EFI), on-the-job training, workshops and mentoring for key staff members on the Audit Procedure Framework and risk-based annual audits. Coaching clinics were operationalized in key areas of the Internal Audit Manual (IAM) and were delivered to the IAD. Such training has increased audit staff's awareness of their role in PFM.

With support from an ADB grant and anchored on extensive training and workshops, the IAD completed its individual three-year rolling Strategic Audit Plans and Annual Audit Plans. The pilot tests were completed successfully in Battambang province and complemented with a study visit to Hanoi, Vietnam. During implementation, the IAD conducted 20 audits of the Provincial Departments of Rural Development, all using the prescribed audit methodology.

To strengthen coordination between the IAD and external NAA and to define cooperation and interface, a dialogue with a World Bank Audit expert at the MEF has been conducted to harmonize the internal audit methodology and ensure a draft audit manual was completed.

Information Systems

The FMIS was installed in MRD in 2018 with usage currently limited to the Department of Supply and Finance. The complete deployment of the system is needed to cover the entire ministry. Many staff members have taken training courses.

Determining the cost of a program requires some type of activity-based costing. This can be very simple or very complicated. The FMIS, once functioning at the required level, will assist in this determination and will be a major benefit to the MRD.

6.3 PFM SYSTEM AT SUBNATIONAL ADMINISTRATION

Subnational Administrations are under the jurisdiction of the General Department of Subnational Administration Finance (GDSNAF) in the MEF. Cambodia has a three-tier subnational government system. According to the 1993 Constitution, the subnational government is divided into two levels: provinces (and capital cities) and municipalities (and district administration). The third level is the Commune Councils (or *Sangkat*), which was established through elections following the 2001 Law on Commune/*Sangkat* Administrative Management. Cambodia has 25 provinces (including the capital), 27 municipalities, 162 districts, 14 Khan (the equivalent of districts for urban areas), 1,405 communes, 241 *Sangkat* (the equivalent of communes for urban areas), and 14,383 villages.

Provincial and district council members are elected indirectly by members of commune councils. The country remains historically centralized. Reforms to decentralize the administration have been ongoing, with the Decentralization and De-concentration Reforms (D&D) launched in 2008 under the supervision of the National Committee for Democratic Development of Subnational Administrations (NCDD) and guided by the 2008 Law on Administrative Management of the Capital, Provinces, Municipalities, Districts, and Khans.

Provinces are in charge of most of the subnational service delivery but remain under the authority of the central government. Communes have political autonomy and independent budget, but only a few mandatory functions, including financial and human resources, have devolved to them. They can deliver services in the following areas: public order and security; management of public services; public welfare; socio-economic development; environment, natural resources and culture; and consultation with resident and community groups. Commune councils may jointly deliver services. Higher levels of government can also delegate some additional responsibilities. Ongoing reforms tend to devolve more functional responsibilities to local government levels.

Subnational governments in Cambodia account for a small share of total public spending. In 2013, the share of government expenditure stood at 3.8 per cent, of which 82.4 per cent was on recurrent expenditure. The small size of the communes limits their capacities to deliver services and their viability as autonomous government units. Most of the funding to communes is spent on staff salaries and small capital projects. Budgeted expenditures of provinces and districts are heavily focused on current expenditures.

The PEFA Report 2015 states that communes/*Sangkat* are provided with firm information on their subsidies for the coming year several months before they complete their budgets. The report also suggests that disbursements follow a fixed schedule with minor delays for communes that fail to submit quarterly accounts on time.

Successes and Challenges

There are no major problems with getting senior staff members in the provincial subnational government to accept PFMRP, although GDSNAF recognizes that there are challenges that occur during the implementation of PFMRP. The implementation of PFMRP requires the provinces to take greater responsibility for doing their job than they had before. It, therefore, takes additional time for them to be prepared and familiar with the technical demands of the reform.

Among all the successes, there are several achievements to be highlighted such as:

- Higher degree of budget and policy linkage through the implementation of the budget strategic plan and performance budgeting.
- FMIS is a key success in budget execution, particularly in producing timely financial reports and keeping track of budget execution.
- Subnational budgets have been increased with a few tax and non-tax revenues being transferred to the subnational level.
- Human resources have been strengthened through various means of teaching and training.
- Subnational Administration Budget System Reform Strategy (BSRS) 2019–25 has been adopted, giving clear direction on how to implement the subnational government finance system in the short, medium, and long term.

The CAP and MAP systems have been working well, but going forward, the process will need improvements in terms of a clear formulation of annual results indicators and cumulative results indicators. Further training is therefore needed to build the capacity of subnational staff members to accommodate the PFMRP.

Budget Creditability

The budget creditability reform stage resulted in a better allocation of funds to the subnational government, from a tiny portion of only 3.8 per cent of the whole government budget in 2013. The Law on Public Financial Management and Budget Strategic Frameworks provide the subnational administrations with technical guidance, a clear roadmap and the legal responsibility for supporting the transfer of resources. However, effective budget allocation requires the integration of budget strategic plans and subnational strategic plans through frequent consultations among relevant actors. Training on how to develop subnational strategic plans that correspond to policy-based budget strategic plans would be helpful to subnational government staff members.

Financial Accountability

The provincial administration is the budget entity with collective provincial technical departments, such as finance and investment. The budget entity is under the direct responsibility of the provincial governor who is the principal authorizer. Currently, a three-year Budgeting Strategic Plan (BSP) is formulated to give direction to the subnational government to prepare its annual budget. Both BSP and PB are subject to review based on the NSDP and the subnational three-year-investment rolling plan.

In addition to NSDP and a three-year-investment rolling plan, the preparation of provincial BSP is guided by an MTBF that defines a budget ceiling for each province administration.

Subnational governments are producing financial statements and reports by budget entities, including monthly, quarterly, and semesterly reports as well as annual financial statements. Most of these reports are prepared on time. They are prepared based on templates attached to the guidelines and circulars. Typically, those reports also need to be verified with relevant entities such as the Department of Treasury to ensure accuracy.

The Internal Audit Department (IAD) is established in the Ministry of Interior (MOI). The procedures for internal audit of the budget entities at the provincial level are defined and implemented by MOI. In addition to the internal audit, there are also financial inspections and external audits to inspect and audit the subnational budget execution.

GDSNAF has been working cooperatively with the FMIS team to enter all subnational budget data and transactions into the FMIS system. Users can get financial information (reports) directly from FMIS. Users may also design their templates to meet their needs by using data and information obtained from FMIS.

6.4 SUMMARY

This chapter discussed the progress and challenges of PFM reforms at the MOEYS and MRD. It also illustrated the structure of PFM systems at the subnational government. The introduction of PFMRP at MOEYS faced some challenges. This included the misconception of the program itself from the beginning as well as staff capacity issues at a later stage. Continued communication and support from MEF and external consultants have produced some positive results.

However, despite its degree, as each ministry has structural differences from one another, some of the systems need to be adjusted to meet the actual need of each ministry. For example, FMIS introduced by MEF could not accommodate the needs of MOEYS due to differences in accounting systems, prompting MOEYS to develop an enhanced version of the Education Management Information System (EMIS). After some periods of adjustments, MOEYS remains a champion of PFMRP in Cambodia.

The Ministry of Rural Development (MRD) leadership strongly supported PFMRP. However, it also experienced a staff capacity issue which will require continuous training for relevant staff members for a certain period. After the training, in general, staff could obtain practical skills in budget preparation and in-year budget prediction in coordination with MEF. This is also true for the usage of FMIS which is currently limited to the Department of Supply and Finance. However, in the future, if the system is expanded to other entities in the ministry, training will be required on an as-needed basis.

The PFMRP of subnational administration is under the jurisdiction of the General Department of Sub-National Administration Finance (GDSNAF) in the MEF. The introduction of the PFM system at the subnational level is a cross-cutting matter involving all ministries in the country. In general, staff members at the provincial level faces more severe capacity issues than those at the central level. However, some of the issues can also be solved if more finance and function are delegated to the subnational level along with the provision of continued training.

NOTE
1. The financial accountability focuses on whether money is spent in the areas for which it was planned. It says nothing about achievement of outputs or outcomes, which are reported under 'performance accountability', which has been defined as the Platform 4 objective.

CHAPTER SEVEN

PFM Experiences of Selected ASEAN and OECD Countries

This chapter highlights public financial management reform experiences of selected ASEAN countries—Thailand, Vietnam, the Philippines, Thailand and Malaysia—and the OECD countries of New Zealand, France, Australia, Sweden and Estonia. It aims to draw lessons and implications for Cambodia's reform program. No one country can provide Cambodia with one specific model to follow that meets its culture and structure of government; therefore, a variety of experiences is the best way to help inform its approach.

7.1 THAILAND: STRATEGIC PERFORMANCE-BASED BUDGETING

Thailand has made impressive strides in social and economic development over the last four decades. Strong, sustained economic growth prompted Thailand to become an upper-middle-income country in 2011[1] and made the country the second-largest economy in Southeast Asia after Indonesia. But before this growth, Thailand suffered a major shock as a result of the Asian Financial Crisis in 1997. The crisis saw the country's annual real GDP rate decline sharply by –1.3 per cent and –9.4 per cent in 1997 and 1998, respectively, down from its 9 per cent growth rate between 1986 and 1996. The crisis taught the country about the huge cost affiliated with weak economic management. It put tremendous pressure on the government's fiscal balance and forced reforms in public sector financial management to enhance public sector efficiency.

As a response to the crisis, the government launched the Public Sector Management Reform Plan (PSMRP). Its vision was for a medium-term institutional transformation to "New Public Management", which focused on improving performance and accountability. The "New Public Management" agenda encompassed five areas: (1) the role, mission and administration of public sector reform; (2) budgets becoming "performance-based"; (3) human resource management reform; (4) legal reform, and (5) value changes.

Performance-based budgeting (PBB) was introduced with a sophisticated framework, a new concept in the Thai public sector. It included the devolution of budget control, a medium-term expenditure framework, a focus on outputs and outcomes, and monitoring and evaluating performance indicators.

Before the reform, Thailand's budget system was centralized, input controlled, inflexible, and distorted by government agencies, which were inefficient in both allocation and operation. The linkages among planning, budgeting, and sectoral policy were weak. The fiscal planning process only focused on annual budgeting, not using a medium-term approach. There was no adequate information technology to support the budget process. Transparency and accountability were also challenging issues. Thailand's budget coverage was incomplete as many extra-budgetary activities[2] were excluded from the annual budget.

To address these issues and enhance allocative and operative efficiency, Thailand adopted performance-based budgeting (PBB), a system that focused on the government agency's performance and output. With technical assistance from the World Bank, a performance-based budgeting framework was introduced with best practices from advanced countries, including New Zealand, the Netherlands, the United Kingdom, the United States and Australia.

In 2000, under the PBB framework, the Bureau of the Budget (BoB) set up a steering committee to work on seven areas of reform including (1) budget planning, (2) output costing, (3) procurement management, (4) budget and funds control, (5) financial and performance reporting, (6) asset management, and (7) internal audit. The seven areas were also known as the "seven hurdles". The reform effort involved reducing controls over line agencies if they achieved hurdle standards. In response to the budget planning hurdle, a Medium-Term Expenditure Framework (MTEF) was introduced. The MTEF aimed at facilitating the link between policy, planning and budgeting, as it allowed BoB to extend its annual budget horizon to be consistent with the five-year National Plan. Therefore, the term "strategic" was added to performance-based budgeting to incorporate the country strategy into the budget formulation, becoming "strategic performance-based budgeting", which was implemented from FY 2003 onward.

In 2002, BoB used a pilot approach by selecting seven government agencies to implement the initial stages of the PBB process. A memorandum of understanding (MOU) was signed between the BoB and the pilot agencies. If the pilot agency cleared the seven hurdles, the BoB would sign a resource agreement. Under the agreement, the BoB would give the pilot agency more fiscal autonomy by providing block grants for the budget allocation at the program level. In addition, the pilot agency and the BoB would collaborate to formulate the pilot agency's medium-term expenditure framework.

However, the implementation of strategic performance-based budgeting had only partial success. In part, this was because of the limited understanding of certain concepts and the absence of a timeframe for pilot agencies to upgrade their standards. Unsatisfied by the slow progress, in 2003, the new government led by Prime Minister Thaksin Shinawatra decided to have every government agency and state enterprise prepare their budget on an output basis and incorporate MTEF as well as activity costing into budget planning.

The sudden universal implementation created numerous difficulties. Pilot agencies lacked a clear understanding of what was required to achieve the new standards. Even among different units within BoB, the understanding of strategic performance-based budgeting and the challenges they faced varied considerably. Many agencies had problems linking planning and budgeting; some agencies were confused about the fundamental concept of strategic planning and could not distinguish between vision and mission.

Most members of Thailand's parliament, especially those with experience in budget reviews, kept examining the budget request on an input-only basis as they felt more familiar and comfortable with it. As a result, the BoB had to work on two budgeting systems in parallel. Therefore, the original intention to move towards the block grant mentioned above has never been reached, in part because of the lack of a mechanism to inform the parliament of the changes in the budgeting system. Furthermore, the MTEF had been providing a medium-term perspective of budget allocation for Thailand, but the medium-term expenditure projections were not used as a base for the following fiscal year budget request.

Notwithstanding the challenges, the reform process resulted in the improved linkage between government strategy and the budget. The BoB is now able to provide the total expenditure on each strategy and policy. Another achievement is the implementation of performance indicators. The focus of public service delivery has expanded to not only quantity but also quality.

The reform momentum was driven by a strong political commitment. It was reinforced and sustained after Thaksin's government announced its Strategic Plan for Thai Public Sector Development, a package of reforms aimed at streamlining public service delivery and increasing overall government efficiency. The concept of New Public Management, which focuses on measurable outputs and outcomes, transparency and responsiveness to the needs of the public, has been used to reform the Thai bureaucracy, and the budget process has been linked to a performance measurement system.

7.2 VIETNAM: PUBLIC INVESTMENT MANAGEMENT

Vietnam has achieved remarkable economic growth in the last three decades and is still one of the fastest-growing economies in the region. The root of this sustainable and rapid growth can be traced back to the drastic reform in 1986, commonly known as *Doi Moi*, transforming the Vietnamese economy from a centrally planned to a market-oriented one. Trade and capital liberalization, privatization of state-owned enterprises (SOEs), and the attraction of foreign firms were key components of economic reforms. As a result, Vietnam's GDP growth jumped from 2.8 per cent in 1986 to 9.5 per cent in 1995 and maintained growth at 7.0 per cent in 2019, although declining in 2009 by 5.3 per cent due to the global financial crisis. Moreover, the poverty headcount declined from nearly 60 per cent in the early 1990s to 20.7 per cent in 2010 and 6.7 per cent in 2018 (World Bank, World Development Indicators Online).[3]

Before the economic reform, Vietnam faced many serious development challenges. Price controls on goods and services became out of control; inflation was running at 700 per cent;[4] high military expenditures and subsidies to state-owned enterprises created pressure for budgetary resources to be used for other essential development expenditures.

While the result of *Doi Moi* has proven to be quite successful, new challenges and complexities have also emerged as the country becomes more modern. Among them, the modernization of the PFM system was critically needed to make sure that the government's revenue mobilization and its expenditures are effective and support economic growth and social development.

Under Vietnam's ongoing reform program, one of the PFM components, public investment efficiency has been identified as an essential driver of future economic development. This reform is urgent due to the rapid declining efficiency of public investment. Capital investments were highly fragmented and not strategically aligned within the Socio-Economic Development Plan (SEDP). The allocation of capital investment lacked strategic prioritization and was spread too thinly across many areas. Plans tended to be over-ambitious, particularly concerning the financial resources available for their implementation. The flow of information to the planning agencies has been less frequent (twice yearly), less reliable and in cumbersome formats, resulting in difficulty in assembling a comprehensive picture of portfolio performance and identifying projects at risk of delivery failure.

Another critical issue comes from the responsibility for PFM in Vietnam, which is split predominantly between the Ministry of Finance (MoF) and the Ministry of Planning and Investment (MPI). The MoF is responsible for revenues, recurrent expenditures, financing, accounting, debt, reporting, and the overall fiscal position. The MPI is responsible for the five-year Socio-Economic Development Plan, procurement, economic forecasting, and capital projects and expenditures. Because of the dual budgeting and planning system, the capital budget is done separately from the recurrent budget causing new projects to be approved without consideration of operational costs to maintain the assets.

Through MPI, the government has made efforts to address this fragmentation by providing stricter provisions in public investment law, which requires all projects to be screened and included in the medium-term investment plan (MTIP). The law has introduced good international practices by moving from an annual capital investment plan to a medium-term horizon. However, the law is not aligned with the rolling medium-term budget plan, an issue that only emerged after the issuance of the State Budget Law (SBL).[5] After the first trial, the MPI sought to revise the public investment law to synchronize with the SBL by moving from the fixed MTIP to a rolling one. The MPI also later initiated the in-house development of an information system for capital budget allocation and monitoring, including projects funded by official development assistance. At the same time, the government has increasingly sought to strengthen public asset management. The 2017 Amendment to the Law on the Management and Use of State Assets offers a strong engagement framework relevant to physical infrastructure and land at the national and subnational levels.

The effort of Public Investment Management (PIM) reform in Vietnam has generated mixed results. Processes for prioritizing expenditures remained ineffective due to the absence of a credible multi-year fiscal framework. Prioritization was carried out separately for capital spending by the MPI and recurrent spending by the MoF, with a significant imbalance between them. The level of capital arrears continued to persist, although the government put a strong emphasis on clearing off the arrears. Some provinces still had a high number of arrears from the past that they could not afford to pay off with the current budget.

The public investment diagnostic conducted by the World Bank in 2017 pointed out the gap between the legal framework, regulations, and practice led to the misallocation of resources and loopholes in the appraisal, budgeting, implementation and evaluation of public investments. The evidence showed that resources were allocated to weak, low-priority, and unaffordable projects. A significant reason behind those challenges is the lack of a well-designed reform program with clear specific objectives and priorities. While the decision to overhaul the public investment management (PIM) system was already made in 2012, no specific reform program has been developed. Effective implementation of the newly promulgated legal documents requires the issuance of detailed guidelines. Public investment is governed by a complex regulatory framework, which includes many laws that remain fragmented.

Nonetheless, with the public investment law, Vietnam introduced a positive paradigm shift in PIM, moving from the traditional annual capital budgeting approach to medium-term financial frameworks to integrate better capital and recurrent expenditures. The shift also aims to strengthen public investment's strategic efficacy, which has been downplayed because of growing decentralization. Medium-term planning and budgeting were introduced to tackle the issues of temporal inconsistencies between the long-term nature of investment and annual budget processes and to improve the predictability of resources available for investment.

The PIM reforms in Vietnam provided some important lessons. The PIM reforms were guided by formal laws without much support to facilitate the transition to the new practice. Legislation needs to be implemented, enforced and well-communicated at the grassroots level. The public investment law by itself cannot change the system and improve PIM. Concerned stakeholders need to be guided and trained on how to implement the laws in practice. Some legislations might also create conflicting ways of doing business, as witnessed between the public investment law and state budget law.

In addition, capacity-building was one of the essential facilitating factors to carry out successful reforms. Training staff to comply with new legislation or use the new system is crucial, especially for staff at the grassroots level. It is also necessary to incentivize the staff to stay at the job after the training through promotions and recognition from the leadership.

7.3 THE PHILIPPINES: DECENTRALIZATION

The Philippines is one of the most dynamic economies in Asia. Its average annual growth increased from 4.5 per cent during 2000–9 to 6.4 per cent during 2010–19. Its gross national income per capita in 2019 was US$3,850 and is steadily on its way to becoming an upper-middle-income country soon. The rapid and sustained economic growth in the Philippines also contributed to overall poverty reduction in the country. The poverty rate decreased from 23.3 per cent in 2015 to 16.6 per cent in 2018.[6]

There are many policy initiatives to engender good governance and sustainable development in the Philippines. Among them is major legislation enacted in 1991, known as the Local Government Code (LGC). This extensive policy aims to strengthen local government capacities so that as front-line governments based at the community level, they can address critical gaps in the service delivery in habitually neglected areas, particularly regarding alleviating poverty and stimulating development activities. The LGC is considered historic legislation as it is comprehensive and extensive, encompassing many aspects of authority devolved to local governments that have not been captured before. It can be seen as a breakthrough, the culmination of the long and difficult journey towards local autonomy in the Philippines.

The Philippines had a strong presidential unitary government system. The national government has three independent branches: the executive, the legislative, and the judiciary. The executive is headed by a popularly elected president. The executive branch is functionally organized into sectoral departments, each headed by a cabinet secretary appointed by the president. The legislature, or Congress, is bicameral and composed of the Senate and the House of Representatives. Senators are nationally elected while representatives are elected by legislative districts. The judiciary is composed of the Supreme Court and the lower courts. As of 2011, the political subdivisions include 80 provinces, 138 cities, 1,496 municipalities, and 41,945 *barangays* (village/neighbourhood level).

Under the LGC, several basic services and facilities have been devolved to local government units (LGUs), including agricultural extension and onsite research, community-based forest projects, field health and hospital services, public works and infrastructure projects, school building programs, social welfare services, tourism facilities, housing projects for provinces and cities, and services about industrial support. For sources of revenue, the LGC authorized locally generated revenues aside from the real property tax, such as taxes on incomes of banks and other financial institutions, forest products and concessions, mines and mineral products, licensing, and permits. The LGUs were also given the authority to adjust tax rates once every five years, but not to exceed 10 per cent of the rates prescribed in the Code, as well as the power to grant tax exemptions. Corollary to this, they are also authorized to borrow from banks and float local bonds without the need of securing authority from the Department of Finance. The LGC also provided for greater citizen participation in local governance with provisions for the mandatory participation and membership of the private sector and non-government organizations in local special bodies, such as local development councils, and local school and health boards.

After twenty-five years of LGC implementation, salutary gains have been recognized:

- Greater involvement of civil society, people's organizations and the private sector in policy-making and the management of public affairs.
- The rise and strengthening of inter-local cooperation through the establishment of leagues of local government units and elected officials.
- Consciousness of the rights of local government units and greater transparency.
- Recognition of best practices under the Galing Pook Awards Program launched as a pioneering awards program recognizing innovation and excellence in local governance.
- Anti-poverty and development initiatives at the local levels.
- Participation in local elections by the citizenry remained strong, if not strengthened. Based on a field appraisal in the different regions of the country in 2015, reports indicated that voter turnout in the communities remained strong, registering as high as 80 per cent.

Furthermore, there are some challenges to be overcome as part of implementation:

- The problem of the absorptive capacities of LGUs has not matched the demands of responsibilities entrusted by the Code. As a large portion of the responsibilities and functions have been devolved to LGUs under the Code, many of these functions require technical skills and preparation that many LGUs in the Philippines may not have.
- Closely related to the problem of absorptive capacities is the dilemma of financial capabilities among LGUs. The principal challenge faced by LGUs is finding the means to mobilize adequate financing for local government.
- Many local governments continue to be dependent on their shares of the internal revenue allotment.[7]
- The National Government continues to hold and control the bulk of productive sources of revenue.

- There is a wide disparity in the distribution of government personnel between the national government and the LGUs.
- Poverty has not been contained, continuing to be endemic even as it has declined during the twenty-five years of Code implementation.
- Political dynasties remain well entrenched in the various provinces, cities and towns of the country, with families controlling elective political offices and positions.

However, it must be noted that decentralization had been a productive force in the Philippines. It marked a turning point in the country's history, and there is a consensus that it has contributed to improvements in development and citizen well-being.

7.4 MALAYSIA: OUTCOME-BASED BUDGETING

Malaysia is one of the most developed countries in the region. It aspires to become a high-income country by 2024. To achieve this milestone, it has to overcome many challenges, especially the so-called "middle-income trap" facing many upper-middle-income economies, which is often due to slow growth in technological advancement and workforce productivity. To support income growth, the Malaysian government needs a sustained and robust fiscal balance so that necessary investments can be carried out.

As part of the reforms to achieve the aforementioned goal, the Malaysian government launched a set of national initiatives. Among them, the National Transformation Program (NTP) launched in 2010 aimed to address key development challenges facing the country. The NTP comprises two main components: The Economic Transformation Program (ETP) and the Government Transformation Program (GTP). The objective of ETP was to elevate the country to developed nation status, while the objective of GTP was to promote a more performance-oriented, accountable, and responsive system of government. As part of the effort, performance-based budgeting (PBB) was adopted by the government. It utilizes an outcome-based budgeting (OBB) approach as a critical part of the strategic reform initiative.

Looking back into the origins of performance-based budgeting, Malaysia was an early leader in Asia in applying performance management to annual budgeting. The program performance budgeting system (PPBS) was introduced in 1969. This system was derived from the United States' approach to program budgeting, with dedicated performance indicators rather than the traditional line-item, input-control approach to budgeting.

Due to the limitations of PPBS and a global trend towards "New Public Management", in 1989, Malaysia introduced a new system called Modified Budgeting System (MBS). However, MBS retained highly centralized controls, which curbed responsiveness, accountability, and flexibility. MBS's initial objective was to devolve managerial and spending powers away from the centre and towards program and project managers, enhancing flexibility and responsiveness. The managers became more accountable for results, articulated through program agreements between line agencies and the Ministry of Finance (MoF) that specified inputs and outputs at the ministry and activity levels. In practice, MBS perpetuated a focus on input utilization. MBS did not adequately support clear linkages between government policies, national planning, and the annual budget process, resulting in its inefficiency as a strategic planning tool.

To address the above issues and other shortcomings of MBS, the Malaysian government decided to adopt a more outcome-based approach to national development planning. This decision became a driver for MoF to seek ways to update the annual budget process. The 10th Malaysia Plan[8] (2011–15) was designed to be outcome-compliant. To that end, the MoF determined that the annual budget would be outcome-focused to strengthen the linkages between policies, planning, and budgeting. Six key transformation levers were identified to guide the development of a new budgeting system: (1) the focus on outcomes, (2) a vertical alignment of national priorities and ministry programs and activities, (3) managing cross-cutting initiatives, (4) coordination of development and operating expenditure, (5) accountability for results and authority over resources, and (6) a systematic monitoring and evaluation (M&E) mechanism.

Outcome-based budgeting (OBB) was created as an integrated results framework at every level of the budget process. Under OBB, the program structures are reviewed and refined through an integrated program-activity structure, which provides hierarchical linkages of ministry programs and activities, and systematically aligns them to national priorities. It also establishes a logical structure on how program information is strategically collected and utilized for planning, budgeting, and M&E. Each program under OBB is aimed at addressing a specific problem.

Conceptually, the OBB system is grounded in a results framework involving top-down strategic planning and alignment, followed by bottom-up budgeting and reporting. The five-year national development plan guides the national-level strategies and priorities. OBB links the different levels—national strategies, ministerial outcomes, program outcomes and activity outcomes—through an integrated results framework. Key performance indicators are defined at each of the subsequent levels of outcomes—ministry, program and activity. On the other hand, performance agreements capture the target outcomes and establish institutional accountability for their achievement at all levels—ministry, program and activity.

In preparation for the design of the OBB, in 2010 the MoF created the National OBB Steering Committee (NOSC), which is a high-level committee to set the policy, guide implementation, and study possible approaches for the new system. An independent unit was also formed—the OBB team—to act as the secretariat to the NOSC and to study the budget systems. The OBB team had the institutional freedom to work full-time on developing the reform. Recognizing the challenges of undertaking reform while also managing core daily tasks, the OBB team was moved to the National Budget Office (NBO) in 2014 to form a new wing called the Performance Management and Evaluation Sector. This team is responsible for supporting, coordinating, and managing the implementation of OBB. This sector is also tasked with developing a systematic M&E framework to complete the full strategic cycle of OBB, as well as with maintaining continuous engagement and capacity building at the NBO and line ministries.

In the first two years (2010–12), five ministries were selected to participate in the pilot program for OBB, with another joining voluntarily, of which MoF was chosen as the core central ministry. After successfully testing the OBB with the original pilot ministries, the OBB team attempted to roll out the system across the whole government. However, there was a low level of understanding of the details of performance budgeting. The results frameworks that were submitted were of low quality, with significant confusion between inputs, outputs, and preliminary, intermediate, and tertiary-level outcomes.

Hence, the OBB team scaled down the scope to focus on three "champion ministries" with whom they could have detailed discussions on how to develop appropriate results chains. This effort has been effectively used as a strategic planning tool in the three champion ministries, leading to additional ministries volunteering in subsequent years. The OBB team has focused on providing specific training and capacity building on a ministry-by-ministry basis to ensure a good understanding of performance management principles and support the development of quality results frameworks. At the central agency level, resource leaders were identified. Resource leaders serve as reference points to advise on OBB matters to line ministries. The OBB team is conducting continuous Resource Leaders Training (RLT) to provide the resource leaders with the necessary conceptual and technical knowledge of OBB. A key feature of Malaysia's change management strategy was the extensive training and awareness-raising program across all levels of stakeholders. At the national level, the OBB team employed a multi-faceted approach with a combination of awareness briefings, forums and seminars, structured training programs, and information sessions. In addition to the national level training, the OBB communication strategy focused on agency-specific training at various levels.

Overall, Malaysia's OBB provides an excellent example of how the strategic planning processes can be linked effectively with budget programs through an integrated results framework. OBB strengthened the focus on outcomes by driving it down to all levels of the central government—from the national level to the ministry level, then to ministry programs and finally to activities. OBB also reinforced accountability for outcomes by establishing performance agreements at the ministry, program, and activity levels.

7.5 INDONESIA: NEW FINANCIAL SYSTEM CALLED SPAN

Indonesia had achieved strong economic performance with an average annual GDP growth of 5.8 per cent in the mid to late 2000s. It later slowed down to 5.3 per cent in 2019.[9] The strong pace of growth has led Indonesia to become an increasingly essential part of the global economy and reach the upper-middle-income country's status in July 2020.[10] Indonesia is now the fourth largest economy in East Asia after China, Japan and South Korea—and the fifteenth largest economy in the world on a purchasing power parity basis.

Strongly hit by the Asian financial crisis of 1997–98, the Indonesian economy contracted by over 13 per cent of GDP in 1998. Government debt reached almost 100 per cent of GDP in 1999. The crisis exposed the lack of efficiency, transparency, and accountability in the management of public resources. This led Indonesia to embark on several ambitious and wide-ranging reform programs, starting in 1998. These reform efforts included amending the constitution, promoting electoral reform, anti-corruption initiatives, public expenditure and revenue management reforms, and decentralization. Many new laws were passed, and new regulatory and monitoring institutions were established, including a powerful Anti-Corruption Commission.

Among all the reforms program, public financial management is part of the government's core reform agenda. It addressed its system's weaknesses, including inadequate accountability, lack of control over state money, overlapping audit institutions, abuse of the system and low-capacity human resources. Decreasing budgetary resources due to the crisis and increasing public expenditure compelled the government to find new ways of using public resources.

In 2001, the Financial Reform Committee was established to respond to the need for reform. The committee played a crucial role in promulgating the Ministry of Finance's (MoF) White Paper on Indonesian PFM.[11] The White Paper articulated the foundation for enacting various laws to modernize the county's financial management system at the central government level.

In 2004, soon after the issuance of new PFM laws and regulations, MoF initiated business process reengineering and capacity-building initiatives to improve efficiency and effectiveness in the management of the state finances. After commencing the PFM reform process, the World Bank has provided financial instruments to strengthen PFM systems in Indonesia. In December 2004, MoF signed a package of loans with the World Bank. It was a combination of credit and grant agreements for the Government Financial Management and Revenue Administration Project (GFMRAP).

The GFMRAP was established to provide support on the overall PFM landscape throughout the widespread reform areas. It is three-phase planning for the implementation over twelve years. Under Phase I, a new financial system, called SPAN,[12] was initiated. SPAN is an automated treasury payment and budget preparation information system aimed at enhancing public efficiency, transparency and accountability. It was initially scheduled to take four to five years to fully implement but eventually took eleven years due to delays in procurement and development of the IT software. Consequently, Phases II and III, dealing with revenue generation, were dropped halfway through to focus on Phase I only.

The deployment of SPAN became the core focus when GFMRAP was first restructured in March 2009. The SPAN contract was worth around US$58.9 million. Of that total, US$46.9 million was funded by the World Bank to finance the supply and installation costs, while the remaining US$12 million was paid from government funds to finance five years of post-warranty and recurrent costs.

During the SPAN project, there were implementation challenges. First, the long delays in the procurement process took almost five years to complete. The procurement of a commercial off-the-shelf (COTS) IT system was a complex activity and the MoF teams had no prior experience with these systems. Secondly, fully elaborating the requirements for the IT system caused seven months of delay. The issue was that SPAN was supposed to assist in the implementation of better business processes that had already been built under a ready-to-use COTS application. However, the ideas about new business processes were not finalized for very long before the software application developer started to work. The improved business processes should have been designed well before developing the software application to allow the processes to be tested in action. A further issue was the significant underestimation of the server capacity required due to greater demands imposed by new business processes and poorly made assumptions in the initial estimates.

However, the strong and continuous commitment from top leadership provided the necessary support for successful reform, despite there having been three Presidents, six Finance Ministers, and some changes with the Director Generals of Treasury and Budget officials over the life of the SPAN Project since 2004. The project commenced with good support from the top management and, despite various challenges, the continuous commitment from the political and bureaucratic levels remained strong enough to complete the project. Ultimately, strong political support was the key to keeping reform moving forward.

Another positive aspect was the strong involvement of the MoF's internal auditor during the project implementation. Their involvement assisted in resolving problems of risk aversion in a climate where civil servants were afraid of making decisions because of tough anti-corruption measures. Change management[13] and adequate communication were also considered important to the outcome of SPAN. Multiple communication media and Change Agent[14] networks were used to help disseminate needed information about SPAN. Finally, a special unit was created to ensure the availability of dedicated full-time staff to manage and implement the SPAN. In 2008, the Directorate for Treasury Transformation was established within the Directorate General for Treasury as a project management unit within the Treasury to oversee all activities related to the development and implementation of SPAN and champion the SPAN reform project effort.

SPAN now manages all financial transactions for more than 24,000 government spending units across Indonesia. Since 2015, SPAN has been operationalized at 222 locations, including 181 treasury branch offices, thirty-three provincial treasury offices, and eight treasury headquarters directorate units. The system's functionality is impressive: it can validate government financial transaction data, control government commitments, support the implementation of accrual-based accounting, and help produce real-time financial reports.[15]

7.6 NEW ZEALAND: OUTCOME-FOCUS MANAGEMENT

New Zealand's public sector management system has been in place for over three decades. The intent of the reforms of the late 1980s and early 1990s was to shift the focus from how much was spent to what it was spent on and why. The core of the model underlying the reforms involves ministers specifying the outcomes they wish to achieve and the outputs (and other interventions) they wish to pursue to achieve these outcomes.

When ministers have agreed on the inputs to be supplied and the parameters they should be provided within, the departments and other providers have the freedom to manage their resources and produce the desired outputs. The other element of the system is an accountability for performance, which is a requirement that managers be held to account for their performance in managing the allocated resources to produce the desired outputs.

Decision-makers need better information than was previously available to make the model work. In particular, as ministers began to focus on outputs rather than inputs, there was a move from cash accounting to accrual accounting. As a result, all stakeholders needed to have more accurate information on how much it cost to produce the desired outputs. At the same time, government budgets began to be presented to parliament in output terms rather than input terms.

An explicit part of the reforms, which relates to the output/outcome distinction, was to outline the separate responsibilities of ministers, at the national level, and chief executives at the subnational level. The approach taken in the New Zealand financial management reforms is to require chief executives to be directly responsible for the outputs produced by their departments, while the ministers choose which outputs should be produced and should therefore have to answer themselves directly for the outcomes. According to the State Sector Act 1988, chief executives are appointed by local councils on three to five-year contracts, with the possibility of renewal, rather than being appointed as permanent heads. This Act also gave chief executives the responsibility for appointing and paying their staff. As stated above, they have the freedom to manage the resources allocated to them for producing desired outputs.

The Fiscal Responsibility Act (1994)[16] requires the government, in the Budget Policy Statement, to specify the broad strategic priorities by which the government will be guided in preparing the budget for that financial year. The strategic priorities have been used as a prioritization tool in the budget process.

The government's high-level goals have been translated into departments' planning through a small number of "key priorities". Previously, key priorities have formed an important part of chief executives' performance agreements. Key priorities were supposed to be defined along the lines of "SMART" goals—Specific, Measurable, Achievable, Results-focused, and Time-bound. Since chief executives were held accountable for delivering on these key priorities, they tended to be outputs rather than outcomes.

Both the budget and departmental planning documents translate strategy into action. The budget contains general output information, but more specific information is contained in an Output Agreement[17] that describes the outputs a department produces within one or multiple years.

Moreover, a key focus for improving outcome information is the policy advice process. This process identifies what the problem is and how to solve or mitigate it. The process requires making judgements, based on evidence and sound reasoning, of how outputs contribute to desired outcomes. The biggest contribution to improved government performance in achieving outcomes is likely to come from improved policy advice based on better information. Several initiatives are underway in this area, which is principally focused on improving the quality of information available on outcomes. This includes work on state indicators at both whole-of-government and the department, levels to define and measure outcomes better. It also requires ensuring that outcomes information is used in decision-making.

Several examples illustrate some of the ways that outcome goals, measures, and targets are used in New Zealand:

- Integrated Offender Management (Department of Corrections): New Zealand's Department of Corrections has been developing a set of outcome measures on the effectiveness of rehabilitative programs for convicted offenders. The programs are intended to reduce recidivism and so reduce the future cost of reincarceration. The effort also contributes to the government's goal of building safer communities. The objective of this outcomes management is to identify the effectiveness of specific rehabilitative programs in reducing recidivism among a targeted group of offenders.
- Road Safety Strategy (Land Transport Safety Authority): The National Road Safety Committee has recently released "Road Safety Strategy 2010". The strategy outlines options for reducing the social costs of vehicular crashes on New Zealand's roads, including public feedback

on which measures to choose. From the perspective of outcomes-focused management, this program is different in that the chosen overall outcome is zero deaths from road crashes, with interventions determined through research and evaluated for success.

- New Zealand Biodiversity Strategy (Department of Conservation): The New Zealand Biodiversity Strategy was released in March 2000 and aimed to halt the decline of New Zealand's indigenous biodiversity. The strategy has a twenty-year timeframe and establishes a framework of goals, objectives and actions required to halt the decline. Priority actions have been identified and implemented that should lead to significant gains in biodiversity over the next five years.
- Maori Education Strategy (Ministry of Education): One of the government's key priorities is to reduce inequalities in health, education, employment and housing. Maori—New Zealand's indigenous people—and Pacific peoples, as a group, fare worse than the population as a whole in these areas. A coordinated effort is underway to reduce these disparities and to ensure that all New Zealanders have the opportunity to participate fully in society. Three areas, in particular, are being targeted: education, employment and health. Outcome measures and targets have been developed for all of them.

The above four examples illustrate that the process in terms of outcome-focus management is well underway, and that it is possible to make progress despite the often-mentioned difficulties in managing outcomes. Considerable effort is being applied to move outcomes into the core of public management practice in New Zealand.

One of the lessons learnt from the New Zealand experience is that creating an environment that enables outcomes-focused management is unlikely to be enough. It is difficult to define, measure and manage outcomes, and in some areas of a government activity, it is probably too difficult. Central agencies must balance the need to be responsive to public input with the need to provide impetus and leadership from the centre. This makes it difficult to drive outcomes-based management from the top-down approach. If agencies are to use outcomes-based systems, they need to have a sense of ownership and so need to develop the tools and systems themselves to fit their businesses.

Moreover, it is important to focus on outcomes in both the internal and external parts of the public management system. While outcomes may have some value in accountability to the public, greater gains may be realized from outcomes in planning, budgeting and decision-making processes. The key is good quality information, particularly on what works and what does not work. In addition, outcome objectives need to be stated and meaningful for both ministers and managers.

Another lesson that can be drawn from the New Zealand experience is that moving the focus to outcomes forces the government to rethink its attitude towards risk. The Department of Corrections (one of the five case studies) example shows that agencies need to be open to the possibility of program failure if they are to improve the effectiveness of government expenditure. The Department of Corrections deliberately allocates a portion of its rehabilitation programs' budgets to test new interventions to assess their effectiveness. Thus, the department can continually improve the value of its expenditure by taking risks and being open to failure.

New Zealand's public service has a large number of specialist agencies. As a result, coordination is critical for effective policy advice and service delivery. Outcomes can play a critical role in focusing agencies on the same issues, and since outcomes often cross organizational boundaries, effective outcome management also requires agencies to coordinate.

Some lessons learnt from the New Zealand case might be:

- it is essential to raise the sense of ownership of government agencies in using outcomes-based systems;
- greater value likely to be realized from outcomes in planning, budgeting, and decision-making processes, than from public accountability; and
- coordination is critical for effective policy advice and service delivery.

7.7 FRANCE: PERFORMANCE BUDGETING

France is one of the most experienced countries in performance budgeting. Its first experiences with performance budgeting were in the 1970s when the French administration applied the US Planning, Programming and Budgeting System. However, it was not successful mainly because it was too theoretical and was disconnected from budget authorizations. In 1990, a new process described by Prime Minister Michel Rocard as "renewal of public service" was put in place based on globalization, contractualization, responsibility and evaluation. This process was not very successful either, but it was useful for introducing performance budgeting, which radically changed the budgetary rule. In 2001, the French parliament unanimously voted to approve the LOLF (*Loi organique relative aux lois de finance*; Organic Financial Law), paving the way for performance budgeting.

In 2006, France moved from line-item to program budgeting. The program budget was structured based on major political objectives. France broke with the tradition of expenditure-oriented budgets by drawing up a program budget with a three-tier structure,[18] in which "missions" correspond to the state's public policy priorities. Each mission comprises programs to which appropriations were allocated, broken down by subprograms, which are the actions that constitute the operational resources for implementing a program. With the LOLF system, each program, whether national or local, has an identified program manager.[19]

The program managers must commit to performance goals. In exchange for their high degree of autonomy, managers must be fully committed to the goals of their programs and be accountable for progress towards results indicators and target values. Performance is measured by three criteria: social and economic effectiveness (outcomes), quality of service and efficiency. The criteria thus reflect the standpoint of citizens, users and taxpayers. Every year, ministers and program managers commit to achieving specific results through an annual performance plan (APP), which is appended to the Budget Act along with the program appropriations requests, the main goals relating to each program, performance indicators and expected results.

In the former system, there was not enough focus on the effectiveness of public spending; instead, the emphasis was on complying with spending authorizations. The newer program-oriented budgets mean that spending departments are accountable to Parliament for their actual expenditures and the quality of what they accomplish. When the budget has been executed, explanations of what was spent and what was accomplished are included in an annual performance report (APR) appended to the Budget Review Act. The APR for the past year must be submitted to Parliament and reviewed before the current year's budget act is passed.

Under the review act, APRs are given to Parliament five months after the end of the fiscal year, and hearings of line ministries are organized by each commission for public discussion, but these sessions are more focused on appropriations and politics than performance results. Nevertheless, some public policies are evaluated in-depth during these sessions depending on each commission's work program. But there is no systematic rolling schedule for regularly evaluating each budget program.

According to the LOLF, the Minister of Finance, in the prime minister's name, presents the budget bill and is responsible for executing the Budget Act. The budget documents show goals and indicators for each program (the APP is appended to the budget bill), and the Central Budget Authority (CBA) is responsible for performance. The CBA must check whether the proposals of goals and indicators that line ministries present adhere to the methodological guide for implementation.[20] However, this debate does not focus enough on results. The discussions between the CBA and line ministries take place in performance conferences, which discuss the choice of indicators and targets and are separate from the budget conferences in which appropriations are negotiated.

Additionally, the APPs express the commitments of the program managers, presenting the strategies and objectives of each program and justifying to Parliament program appropriations. Program managers organize management control in conjunction with those responsible for the Program Operating Budgets (BOPs). In return, they are allocated an overall amount to control. This gives them a great deal of freedom to choose where and how to allocate the financial and human resources they have available to meet their objectives. Their choices and effects are reported in the APRs. There are about eighty program managers in the general state budget, who are secretaries-general or central administration directors. Of these, 60 per cent are responsible for a single program each, the others for two or three.

However, along with the successes, there are several challenges related to the performance budget system:

Capacity and recourse to cover transaction costs: Because of the general budget constraints, allocating resources to performance is not a priority. For one thing, it has created a managerial bureaucracy parallel to the traditional bureaucracy. Its implementation could produce increased rigidity and strengthening of constraints in the preparation and conduct of budgets and lead to the de-motivation of managers.

Too many measures, or too few? In 2006, the LOLF's first year, the APRs presented 650 objectives and 1,300 indicators for the general budget, however, by 2015, these figures had been almost halved. Parliament itself is complaining about the amount of information it must contend with, which has substantially increased since 2005. The number of budgetary document pages has increased from 3,500 for the last line-item budget to 14,000 today.

Evaluating data trustworthiness: Line ministry data come mainly from the ministry statistics services, staffed by civil servants trained in the traditionally independent French Statistics Service, or from opinion polls that have been audited. But no one in either the line ministries or the Budget Department is in charge of checking data quality. This job has devolved to the Inter-Ministerial Program Audit Committee, the independent structure of inspectors that guarantees the relevance and reliability of the information in the APPs. Criticisms were made about frequent changes of indicators in the early years of LOLF that were not reported in the APPs.

Erosion of political support: The economic crisis that began in France in 2008 as a consequence of the Lehman Brothers' failure and the subsequent sovereign debt crises have changed the priorities of the French government. Encouraging better performance has given way to the search for budgetary savings. Performance has not been abandoned, but there are no more illusions about getting quick results.

Creating cross-cutting goals: Central government programs usually represent the appropriations and goals related to the main public policies. Nevertheless, some public policies can be implemented by more than one line ministry and the appropriations may be located in several programs. To set out in detail the goals of policies whose appropriations are fragmented into different programs, the budgetary "cross-cutting policies document" contains the common goals and indicators for each public policy.

Variations in the use of performance data: Defining indicators is more delicate in the public than in the private sector because it implies successfully measuring effects that are not financial, and it contradicts traditional financial control modes. To limit these negative effects, the role of performance indicators should be thought of not only in terms of control and incentives but also as topics for discussion and the exchange of good practices.

In terms of the civil service culture, the LOLF has been a success. The Financial Committee of the National Assembly wrote in a 2011 report, "No doubt one of the most important successes of the LOLF after five years ... is the dissemination of a performance culture and management in the French civil service, thanks to the chain of accountability." That same year, the State Audit Office said in the tenth-anniversary report, "The performance culture has been broadly disseminated among public servants."

It is clear that improvements are needed in several areas:

- a better selection of strategic mission indicators;
- standardization of efficiency indicators for support services;
- harmonization of common indicators for several programs; and
- methods for checking the reliability and consistency of measurements and indicators over time.

The main challenge is to continue to reduce the number of indicators to guarantee that both ministers and members of Parliament have a better understanding of performance. There is not as yet enough political ownership by the executive or the legislature. Performance budgeting is a gradual process that takes time because it is an iterative and continuous improvement process.

7.8 AUSTRALIA: PERFORMANCE BUDGETING

Australia is one of the very few countries with more than thirty years of experience in performance budgeting. In 2015, the approach to performance budgeting went into a transition due to the promulgation of the Public

Governance, Performance and Accountability Act (PGPA Act). This new law not only merged and refined previous financial management laws covering government departments, but it also introduced the concept of "performance" into legislation.

At the national level in Australia, the link between performance and budgeting has lacked specifics. Annual appropriations for a program or outcome had been associated with objectives, results, and deliverables, but were rarely tied to a specific quantity or other output. In some instances, resource agreements for demand-driven activities have been negotiated based on unit costs. The Department of Finance (DOF) introduced new guidance defining performance in the context of information relating to the efficiency and effectiveness of activities and the achievement of an entity's purpose. The guidance states that key performance indicators may not even be the best way to monitor the results of an activity, especially where it is difficult to measure the impact in quantitative terms. It suggests a range of other tools that can be used, among them benchmarking, stakeholder surveys, peer reviews, and comprehensive evaluations.

To look back at the change in Australia's performance budgeting over time, the performance framework can be traced directly to a 1983 parliamentary review of government administration. The review illustrated an urgent need for a more efficient and cost-effective public sector. The government's response was to introduce a broad reform that covered many aspects of public administration and encompassed fundamental changes to budgeting and accountability, including the introduction of program-based appropriations and medium-term expenditure plans.

The performance agenda was a vital component of the Financial Management Improvement Plan (FMIP), established as a part of the government initiative for public administration reform. A cross-agency steering committee oversaw the FMIP, and every two years reported to Parliament on progress. A common theme in all the reports and the Parliamentary review of FMIP in 1990 was the need for better-quality information about performance. Refinements were made to FMIP incrementally to strengthen the use of performance indicators for each program, moving towards outcome-focused indicators rather than activities, and introducing a comprehensive program evaluation regime for all budget-funded entities. All programs had to be evaluated within five years and the DOF reviewed the evaluation plans and provided extensive training, support, and monitoring of evaluations.

The change of government in 1996 brought in an administration that was keen to adopt more of a private-sector culture. The idea that governments could establish a quasi-market[21] for public services defined by fully priced outputs that could be purchased from the source, and which provided the best value for the money spawned a revised model for budgeting. Specific dimensions of performance became mandatory in budget planning, reporting to Parliament, and accounting for results in annual reports. This included outputs by price, quantity and quality, and outcomes with specific indicators and targets. The evaluation was considered to be part of the responsibility of line entities for delivering quality outputs and outcomes. The central role of the DOF in supporting and monitoring evaluations was discontinued.

The concept of outputs was eventually dropped in 2010 with the reintroduction of programs that were less comprehensive than the FMIP programs. The new programs were intended to provide a clearer basis for resource allocation and accountability that was more meaningful to stakeholders, especially Parliament. They were also supposed to strengthen the link between government actions and the outcomes. However, when the introduction of programs did not effectively address the performance system's perceived weaknesses, in 2012, the administration embarked on another endeavour to improve the transparency of performance and accountability for results. The Commonwealth Financial Accountability Review involved extensive consultation on various issues and reform options, culminating in the PGPA Act.

The Act was passed in 2013 but it took almost two years for regulations and guidance to be drafted, and it is still too early to comment on their efficacy or impact as very little of the enhanced framework has been implemented. The guidance implies that the expectations for more extensive evaluation and review anticipated in the PGPA Act will lead to more transparent performance. A further implication is that the expected heightened scrutiny will result in more action to improve performance.

Establishing and maintaining performance information has been seen as a normal cost of operations to be funded within the overall allocations for administration; however, there has been very little training and skills development by the centre. Guidance and a short period of central training were provided after the outcomes and outputs arrangements were introduced, but minimal new guidance and support were provided to line agencies to improve their quality and address situational challenges. There has also been little concern for quality assurance or any focus on ensuring that information is used effectively.

The Australia National Audit Office identified as continuing major challenges to developing meaningful performance indicators: (1) the limitations of a homogeneous framework for a diverse range of functions and activities; (2) difficulties in providing coherent reporting on multi-agency activities; (3) bridging the gap between actions and outcomes; (4) difficulties in measuring efficiency and clearly defined outcomes; and (5) the need for more rigorous independent assurance arrangements for entity performance reporting.

In conclusion, as the most recent changes to Australia's public performance regime are not yet fully in place, it is not possible to extract any lessons from practical experience with the changes. Instead, it is necessary to seek the lessons from the reasons for those changes and the differences that they are expected to make. The main changes in performance arrangements since 2013 have been made to give greater emphasis to entity-level planning and the integration of performance goals in mandatory corporate plans. These changes have been reinforced by a new format for reporting on progress towards those goals. The link between performance and budgets has been revised to reduce the amount of performance information in budget-related reports.

7.9 SWEDEN: GENDER BUDGETING

Sweden has a long history of promoting women's opportunities for economic independence; it is a central tenet of its gender equality policy. Some of the most significant reforms for gender equality took place within the labour market and in social policy since the 1970s. Women gained access to employment and greater financial independence, which increased their well-being and bargaining power in the household.

The first reform was the separate income taxation (1971), meaning that husband and wife were taxed individually and not jointly. This created an incentive for women to work as their income was no longer seen as part of the husband's income. The second reform was the introduction of parental allowance, introduced in 1974, and entitled both husband and wife to parental leave. The third major reform was the development of public childcare, which allowed more women to be employed. These reforms are the result of various forces, not simply a push for greater gender equality; there was also a great demand for labour in Sweden in the 1970s.

Forty years later, the new government elected in 2014 declared itself a feminist government and outlined its intention to institute gender budgeting in the government. Currently, the annual budget circular includes instructions on applying gender budgeting throughout the budget process. One of the requirements is that gender impact analysis is carried out at the early stage of new budget proposals. The government provides a clear statement of gender-related objectives and each proposal in the Budget Act is accompanied by a gender impact assessment.

In this effort, Sweden created a Minister for Gender Equality, with responsibility for policy implementation and development, as well as for anti-discrimination and anti-segregation. This minister has the same autonomous power and authority as other ministries. Further tasks of this minister are coordination, development and follow-up of gender mainstreaming, which requires all government ministers to take a gender equality perspective in their decisions. Each ministry has a Gender Equality Coordinator, who is part of an inter-ministerial working group on gender mainstreaming that meets quarterly.

In 2018, the government established the Swedish Gender Equality Agency to contribute to the effective implementation of gender equality policy. One of the agency's key tasks is the systematic follow-up and analysis of progress towards the achievement of gender equality policy. The agency's work requires cooperation with other government agencies, municipalities, county councils, enterprises and industry. Each year, the Gender Equality Agency presents, collects and analyses the measures adopted by relevant government agencies to reach Sweden's gender equality goals. According to the 2016 OECD Survey of Gender Budgeting, Sweden is one of twelve OECD countries that has introduced gender budgeting to date.

Despite progressive gender equality policies, Sweden is still marked by differences in employment and income between women and men. For example, in 2015, 76.8 per cent of women aged 20 to 64 years were gainfully employed compared to 79.0 per cent of men, and women earned just 94 per cent of the standard weighted salary of men.

Nonetheless, gender equality has contributed to Sweden's high levels of employment and growth. However, it has not happened by itself; it is largely the result of political will. There needs to be a commitment to creating fair and gender-equal conditions for women and men, girls and boys. The Swedish government will continue to enhance gender budgeting, to ensure that this policy will contribute to gender equality. A feminist government's policy agenda must be paired with the allocation of resources and a true commitment to making a change.

7.10 ESTONIA: E-GOVERNMENT

Estonia is a small nation with a population of approximately 1.3 million people. After its independence from the Soviet Union in 1991, Estonia moved aggressively towards the digital economy by adopting technological innovation as a growth strategy of the nation. Estonia uses information technology as an instrument for increasing administrative capacity and ensuring an innovative and convenient living environment for citizens. Estonia is considered one of the most advanced information technology societies in the world due to its efficient, secure and transparent digital ecosystem. With over twenty years of expertise and experience in automating public and private sector services, Estonia today has shared its e-governance journey with sixty governments and exported its solutions to over 130 countries around the world.

After independence, Estonia was left with minimum resources and infrastructure. However, it has quickly established the foundation necessary to implement the e-Estonia initiative and strategies. The policy instruments were tackled early on, including a policy and regulatory framework; institutionalization and governance; a technical infrastructure for interoperability; public-private partnerships for promoting businesses and start-ups; competencies and education that place significant emphasis on digital literacy at all levels; and safe data sharing among institutions.

Moreover, several crucial components have facilitated Estonia's reliance on the Internet. First, the "Electronic ID Card" enables users to securely verify their identity and thus gain access to online systems. Since e-ID cards are issued to every Estonian over the age of 15, 90 per cent of citizens use this digital identification system constantly. Second, the "X-Road" project was launched by the Estonian government in the 1990s to create a secure and standardized environment for interconnection, enabling data exchange between a multitude of different information systems, which has allowed the creation of various innovative e-solutions. Third, the existence of "public Wi-Fi" throughout Estonia, even in less populated areas, enables all citizens to have constant access to each of the nation's online programs. Finally, the Estonian national cybersecurity arrangements allow public and private sectors and citizens to interact securely in a common data exchange environment while ensuring confidentiality and privacy. The result is that Estonia has thousands of e-services, which are accessible worldwide. These mechanisms have permitted Estonia to develop extensive systems that have enhanced government operations by eliminating some bureaucratic barriers, improving quality of life, and creating thousands of jobs, particularly in the information technology sector.

At present, a great deal of daily life is done digitally, from filing taxes to paying for parking. In school, a child's attendance, homework and grades are all available online. Residents can pay for parking through their mobile phones or reserve time slots for passing border checkpoints. Nearly all citizens file their taxes online through the E-Tax electronic tax filing system, which only takes an average of three to five minutes to complete. Health records are digitized, while residents can sign legally binding contracts online or register a business. Business owners can also check their property and legal records online. One can even apply for an e-Residency digitally. Estonia also has one of the fastest Internet connection speeds globally, the result of fibre-optic cabling established throughout the country in the early 2010s. Wi-Fi is available free of charge throughout the country.

e-Estonia has realized significant savings and efficiencies. The government saves 2 per cent of state GDP with the use of digital signatures alone. Linking up thousands of databases saves about 820 years of working time for the state and citizens annually. Regarding e-Government, 98 per cent of Estonians have a national ID card, over 25,000 people have applied for e-Residency, and over 30 per cent of Estonian voters from 116 countries use i-Voting in Estonian elections. Police work has become fifty times more effective, and e-Police systems are available in police cars uniting over fifteen databases, including those of Schengen and Interpol.

The Estonian experience has shown that a successful information society based on e-solutions can be built safely without compromising privacy. However, institutional leaders are required to take on new challenges as it is necessary to provide citizens with training on the benefits and advantages of digitization. The success of e-governance has helped Estonians enjoy a wide range of e-solutions and the model has become a paradigm for others who wish to follow the same path.

Critical factors that a state should consider in digitizing itself include:

- "once-only" or collecting data only one time by any institution, eliminating duplicated data and bureaucracy;
- interoperability to ensure that all system elements exchange data securely and work smoothly together;
- digital identity to allow authentication without physical contact; and
- cross-border services that provide data exchange with other nations.

Another crucial feature of the Estonian digital infrastructure is its transparency: any citizen can log in to their government interface and see who has enquired information about them, whether it is a police officer, a doctor they visited, or a tax official.

The lesson of Estonian digital transformation success is a lesson on trust and transparency. Any company or organization, which looks into digital transformation and innovation, has to rely on its customers', members' or employees' trust for the initiative.

7.11 LESSONS LEARNT

Thailand adopted Strategic Performance-Based Budgeting in 2003. Even though its government has a strong political commitment to performance budgeting, civil servants' readiness for implementation is also necessary for success. As it moves to performance-informed budgeting, Cambodia has introduced the Communication and Engagement Strategy, an important tool to help civil servants to be ready for the new budget system. The similar challenges encountered by Thailand hold a lesson Cambodia has learnt.

Vietnam introduced the Public Investment Law (2014) to address some fragmentation in Public Investment Management. The law by itself cannot change the system and improve public investment management, relevant stakeholders need to be guided and trained on how to implement the law. Cambodia has introduced the Public Investment System Reform Strategy 2019–25, formulating a series of legal documents that establish the principles and management systems needed for implementation. The government has provided workshops and training to stakeholders, but further guidance, as well as monitoring and evaluation, will be needed to improve organizational capacity and ensure the objectives of this reform strategy are achieved.

The Philippines enacted the Local Government Code in 1991 which devolved many powers and authorities to local governments. It marked a turning point in the country's history and has contributed to improvements in development and citizen well-being. However, the Philippines encountered challenges from capacity constraints in implementation. Cambodia has, through de-concentration and decentralization, also transferred functions and resources to its subnational administrations. Similarly, it faces the challenges of capacity constraints as well as issues in resource allocation. Devolution requires both capacity-building at the local level and clear guidance from the centre.

Malaysia, since 2010, has introduced outcome-based budgeting (OBB), a critical part of its strategic reform initiatives. Malaysia's OBB, addressing the encountered challenges, provides an excellent example of how strategic planning processes can be linked effectively with budget programs through an integrated results framework. Cambodia can learn from the Malaysian experience by finding "champion ministries" to lead implementation.

Indonesia has demonstrated an excellent integrated financial management system—SPAN—that has benefited from the strong and continuous commitment of top leadership. Similarly, the Minister of Economy and Finance in Cambodia showed strong leadership and high commitment to moving the FMIS to a successful start.

The budget management system in New Zealand has focused on outcomes since the reforms of the late 1980s. The core of this model involves ministers specifying the outcomes they wish to achieve and the outputs that are needed to create them. For Cambodia, raising the sense of ownership in this way will allow for greater gains in implementing performance budgeting and planning.

France's first experiences with performance budgeting were in the 1970s when the French administration applied some aspects of the US system. Cambodia can learn from the French experience in implementing performance budgeting, particularly about the selection of strategic indicators, the standardization of efficiency indicators, and the reliability and consistency of indicators over time.

Australia's lesson for Cambodia is to include greater emphasis on entity-level planning and the integration of performance goals in agency planning. There is also a need to reduce the amount of unnecessary performance information in budget-related reports.

Like Sweden, Cambodia has made gender equity and women's empowerment major policy agendas of the Royal Government reflected in the Cambodian national development goals.

Estonia has an impressive practice in e-government that should inspire Cambodia as to what is possible. While Cambodia is far from Estonia in the IT sector, its success shows the potential this sector can have in moving its government and its country forward.

NOTES

1. Refer to https://www.worldbank.org/en/news/press-release/2011/08/02/thailand-now-upper-middle-income-economy
2. The term "extra budget activities" generally refers to sets of government transactions that are not included in the annual budget presentation.
3. World Bank, "World Development Indicators" database (accessed 10 January 2021).
4. This happened in the mid-1980s during the launching of *Doi Moi*. Refer to http://factsanddetails.com/southeast-asia/Vietnam/sub5_9g/entry-3470.html
5. The State Budget Law 1996 was later revised in 2015.
6. Ruth Abbey Gita Carlos, "Pernia Sees 10 to 12% Poverty Rate in PH by 2022", *Philippine News Agency*, 11 December 2019, https://www.pna.gov.ph/articles/1088478
7. The Internal Revenue Allotment (IRA) is the main transfer program, which

shares 40 per cent of internal revenues through a clearly defined formula. These resources are considered a block or unconditional grant.
8. A comprehensive outline of government development policies and strategies; also referred to as Malaysia's 5-Year Plan. The first plan was introduced in 1965, covering the development agenda from 1966 to 1970. Refer to https://www.igi-global.com/dictionary/government-malaysia-barriers-progress/17730
9. "World Development Indicators" database, https://data.worldbank.org/indicator/NY.GDP.MKTP.KD.ZG?locations=ID (accessed 10 January 2021).
10. Refer to https://www.indonesia-investments.com/news/news-columns/economic-update-indonesia-world-bank-upgrades-indonesia-to-upper-middle-income-country/item9308
11. The 2002 White Paper highlighted the need for comprehensive PFM reforms covering budget preparation and execution, revenue administration, public accounting and auditing, and accountability for results to the Parliament and the people.
12. SPAN is an abbreviation of *Sistem Perbendaharaan dan Anggaran Negara*, which means Integrated Financial Management Information System (IFMIS).
13. Change management is defined as the process of helping people understand the need for change, and to motivate them to take actions which result in sustained changes in behaviour.
14. Change Agents were formally recruited and trained to act as information providers and opinion leaders within their work units, keeping their colleagues updated on implementation.
15. Refer to https://www.indonesia-investments.com/finance/financial-columns/world-bank-span-improves-indonesia-s-efficiency-transparency-accountability/item6557
16. The Fiscal Responsibility Act passed the National Assembly in 1994, reflecting the advice of the Treasury to improve the transparency of budget decision making.
17. Previously it was called "purchased agreement". The minister becomes the purchaser of agreed outputs from the department, and chief executives are held accountable for their production in (since 1993) purchase agreements signed by the chief executive and the minister.
18. The three-tier structure of program budget comprises mission, program and subprogram.
19. For each program, the minister appoints a manager. Program managers are the linchpin of the new public management system, operating at the nexus between political and management accountability.
20. To reach political consensus on what constitutes performance, the CBA has written a methodological guide that has been signed off on by the Ministry of Finance (MoF), the chairman of the financial committee and the general

rapporteur of the budget of each Assembly, the chairman of the State Audit Office, and the president of the Inter-ministerial Committee of Program Audit.
21. A quasi-market is a public sector institutional structure that is designed to reap the supposed efficiency gains of free markets without losing the equity benefits of traditional systems of public administration and financing.
22. Donald Moynihan and Ivor Beazley, "Toward Next Generation Performance Budgeting: Lessons from the Experiences of Seven Reforming Countries", in *Direction in Development, Public Sector Governance* (World Bank, 2016), https://openknowledge.worldbank.org/bitstream/handle/10986/25297/9781464809545.pdf

Bibliography

Andrews, M. 2014. "Why Distributed End Users Often Limit Public Financial Management Reform Success". *CID Working Paper*, no. 283.

Asian Development Bank. 2001. "What is Public Expenditure Management (PEM)?". *The Governance Brief*, issue 1-2001. https://www.adb.org/sites/default/files/publication/28648/governancebrief01.pdf (accessed December 2020).

de Renzio, Paolo, and Joachim Wehner. 2017. "The Impacts of Fiscal Openness". *World Bank Research Observer*, Vol. 32 (2): 185–210.

Diamond, Jack. 2012. *Guidelines for Sequencing PFM Reforms*.

Gita-Carlos, Ruth Abbey. 2019. "Pernia Sees 10 to 12% Poverty Rate in PH by 2022". *Philippine News Agency*, 11 December 2019. https://www.pna.gov.ph/articles/1088478

Hudson, D., and A. Leftwich. 2014. "From Political Economy to Political Analysis". *Developmental Leadership Program, Research Paper* 25.

Hughes, C., and J. Hutchison. 2012. "Development Effectiveness and the Politics of Commitment". *Third World Quarterly* 33, no. 1: 17–36.

International Budget Partnership. 2014. "From Numbers to Nurses: Why Budget Transparency, Expenditure Monitoring, and Accountability are Vital to the Post- 2015 Framework". *Budget Brief*, October 2014. https://www.internationalbudget.org/wp-content/uploads/Budget-Brief-From-Numbers-to-Nurses.pdf

International Labour Organization. 2018. "How Has Garment Workers' Pay Changed in Recent Years". *Cambodian Garment and Footwear Sector Bulletin*, Issue 7, June 2018.

International Monetary Fund. 2012. "Fiscal Transparency, Accountability, and Risk". IMF: Washington, DC. http://www.imf.org/external/np/pp/eng/2012/080712.pdf

———. 2019. *Artcle IV Consultation*. Washington, DC.

Ministry of Economy and Finance. 2020. *Cambodian Public Debt Statistic Bulletin* Vol. 9, Data as of Year-end 2019, issued in March 2020. p. 3.

Moynihan, Donald, and Ivor Beazley. 2016. "Toward Next Generation

Performance Budgeting: Lessons from the Experiences of Seven Reforming Countries". In *Direction in Development, Public Sector Governance*. World Bank. https://openknowledge.worldbank.org/bitstream/handle/10986/25297/9781464809545.pdf

Overy, Neil. 2011. "In the Face of Crisis: The Treatment Action Campaign Fights Government Inertia with Budget Advocacy and Litigation". *International Budget Partnership*, Case Study Series No. 7, August 2011. https://www.internationalbudget.org/publications/in-the-face-of-crisis-the-treatment-action-campaign-fights-government-inertia-with-budget-advocacy-and-litigation/

Royal Government of Cambodia. 2019. *Report of PFM and TWG Meeting on 2019 Progress Report of PFM Reform Program Stage 3*.

———. 2020. *Report of Mid-term Budget Execution Evaluation and Estimation of Implementing 2020 Budget Law*.

Sarr, Babacar. 2015. "Credibility and Reliability of Government Budgets: Does Fiscal Transparency Matter?". *International Budget Partnership, Working Paper* no. 5. Washington, DC. http://www.internationalbudget.org/publications/credibility-and-reliability-of-government-budgets-does-fiscal-transparency-matter/

Sjoberg, Fredrik Matias, Jonathan Mellon, Tiago Carneiro Peixoto, Johannes Zacharias Hemker, Lily Lee Tsai. 2019. "Voice and Punishment: A Global Survey Experiment on Tax Morale". *World Bank Group Policy Research Working Paper* 8855.

Slocomb, M. 2010. *An Economic History of Cambodia in the Twentieth Century*. Singapore: NUS Press.

Touchton, Michael, and Brian Wampler. 2014. "Improving Social Well-Being through New Democratic Institutions". *Comparative Political Studies* 47(10): 1442–69.

———, Brian Wampler, and Tiago Peixoto. 2019. "Of Governance and Revenue Participatory Institutions and Tax Compliance in Brazil". *World Bank Group Policy Research Working Paper* 8797. https://openknowledge.worldbank.org/bitstream/handle/10986/31492/WPS8797.pdf

Wildavsky, A. 1986. *Budgeting: A Comparative Theory of the Budgetary Processes*. New Brunswick and Oxford: Transaction Publishers.

World Bank Group. 1999. *Cambodia—Public Expenditure Review Enhancing the Effectiveness of Public Expenditures: Summary*. World Bank Group. https://policycommons.net/artifacts/1516995/cambodia-public-expenditure-review-enhancing-the-effectiveness-of-public-expenditures/2194234/ (accessed 28 December 2022).

World Bank. 2014. *Problem-Driven Political Economy Analysis: The World Bank Experience*, edited by V. Fritz, B. Levy, and R. Ort. Washington, DC.

———. 2017. *Political Economy of Public Financial Management Reforms: Experiences and Implication for Dialogue and Operational Engagement.*
———. 2021. *World Development Indicators.* https://data.worldbank.org/country/cambodia (accessed May 2021).

Glossary

Technical Term	Meaning/Description
Accommodation Tax	Tax imposed on accommodation in hotels and guest houses at the rate of 2 per cent and is collected by the person who supplies accommodation services.
Advance Ruling	A written statement issued by the GDCE to a person upon his/her written request on (1) the tariff classification, (2) the interpretation and application of the Law and regulations relating to the customs valuation, or (3) the origin of the goods to be imported. The advance rulings are binding on the Customs from the effective date of the ruling.
Annual Budget Law	To be enacted prior to the year to which it refers. All revenues and expenditures are included in the budget on a gross basis.
Ad hoc	When necessary or needed.
Allocation Efficiency	The assurance of allocation on target.
Accountability	An obligation or willingness to accept responsibility or to account for one's actions from Line Ministries or entities, subnational administration. Components of strengthening accountability are: (1) objective can be measurable and specific responsibility; (2) prepare plans in order to achieve the goal; (3) implement the action and monitor the progress; (4) report the progress; (5) outcome evaluation and feedback.
Arrears	Payables that have remained unpaid after a specified number of days (60 days) after the date on the invoice or contract, in accordance with a law, regulation, government payment policy or local practice. Payment not made by the due date.

Audit-based Performance Framework	An independent and objective assessment of an entity's activities, program, processes, internal controls systems, governance and risk management, with regard to one or more of the three aspects of economy, efficiency and effectiveness of resource used, aiming to lead to improvements.
Accrual Accounting	An accounting method that records revenues and expenses when they are incurred, regardless of when cash is exchanged. The term "accrual" refers to any individual entry recording revenue or expense in the absence of a cash transaction.
Accounting System	The system used to manage the income, expenses, and other financial activities of a business. There are 2 Accounting Systems—Cash Accounting and Accrual Accounting.
Authorized Economics Operator (AEO)	A party that is involved in the international movement of goods in whatever function that has been approved by or on behalf of a national Customs administration as complying with World Customs Organization (WCO) or equivalent supply chain security standards.
Agreement Establishing the ASEAN-Australia-New Zealand Free Trade Area (AANZFTA)	The legal text that set outs the obligations and commitments of the Parties to the Agreement (chapter-by-chapter listed here): Chapter 1: Establishment of Free Trade Area; Chapter 2: Trade in Goods; Chapter 3: Investment
Bank Reconciliation	In bookkeeping, it is a process by which the bank account balance in an entity's books of account is reconciled to the balance reported by the financial institution in the most recent bank statement. Any difference between the two figures needs to be examined and, if appropriate, rectified.
Budget Credibility	The ability of governments to meet their expenditure and revenue targets accurately and consistently. At its core, budget credibility is about upholding government commitments and seeks to understand why governments deviate from these commitments.
Budget Comprehensive	A compilation of an operating budget explaining all revenues, expenses and capital expenditures for short-term annual goals involving recurring items.
Budget Discipline	The extent to which the Ministry of Economy and Finance is able to forecast cash commitments and

	requirements and to provide reliable information on the availability of funds to budgetary units for service delivery.
Budget Entity	A unit or function at the lowest level to which funds are specifically appropriated in the appropriations act.
Budget Expenditure	The estimated expenditure of the government during a given fiscal year.
Budget Framework	Fiscal arrangements that allow the government to extend the horizon for fiscal policy-making beyond the annual budgetary calendar. In Cambodia, the horizon is 3 years.
Budget	An estimate of income and expenditure for a set period.
Blueprint	A design plan or other technical drawing that can be used to specify a plan.
Citizen Budget	A simplified version of a Finance Act intended for all citizens to be informed of the multi-annual macroeconomic and budgetary outlook, new fiscal measures, general expenditure guidelines, sectoral priorities in relation to the public Investment program, and measures taken for regional development.
Civil Society	A group of people that operates in the community and that is not part of the government or a business; includes non-governmental organizations and social movements.
Commitment	A contractual obligation to make a future payment when a service is delivered in the future. The obligation is not recognized as a liability.
Compliance	The fulfilment of tax obligations by businesses and individuals. The four main categories of taxpayer obligations prescribed in tax laws are: (1) registration in the tax system; (2) timely filing of declarations; (3) payment of tax liabilities on time; and (4) complete and accurate reporting of information in tax declarations.
Consistency	Consistency in the pattern of behaviour, agreement, harmony, or compatibility, especially correspondence or uniformity among the parts of a complex thing.
Capacity Development Plan	The development of a clear and practical plan, with a timeline, measurable indicators and a

	realistic budget, to address capacity needs identified through an assessment. The plan should set out the capacity objectives, activities and indicators; and the resources required to implement change and to measure progress.
Cash Management	A broad area of finance involving the collection, handling and usage of cash.
Classification of the Functions of Government	Developed by the OECD, the Classification of the Functions of Government (COFOG) classifies government expenditure data from the System of National Accounts by the purpose, for which the funds are used.
Chart of Account (CoA)	A listing of the names of the accounts that a company has identified and made available for recording transactions in its general ledger.
Check and Balance Mechanism	A system that allows each branch of a government to amend or veto acts of another branch to prevent any one branch from exerting too much power.
Tax Revenue	Revenues collected from taxes on income and profits, social security contributions, taxes levied on goods and services, payroll taxes, taxes on the ownership and transfer of property, and other taxes.
Tax Declaration	A standard form provided by the tax administration on which a taxpayer reports information relating to a core tax liability. Also called a tax return.
Tax Dispute	Disputed tax assessments normally arise: (a) from administrative error; or (b) as an outcome of a tax audit or investigation that has identified a discrepancy that is disputed by the taxpayer on grounds of facts or legal interpretation. TADAT assessments focus on (b). Tax laws typically provide for a formal dispute mechanism.
Tax Evasion	Deliberate acts to conceal income in order to escape tax liabilities (e.g., hiding money in secret offshore bank accounts).
Tax on Salary	A monthly tax imposed on a salary that has been received within the framework of fulfilling employment activities by both resident and non-resident physical persons and is withheld by the enterprise/employer of the employees.
Tax on Property Rental	Tax collected from the proprietors or assignees on the rental of properties such as buildings, manual tools

	equipped with industrial institutions, Industrial and commercial installed fittings, floating houses, ships used as accommodations or for business services, and free land (land without buildings).
Transparency	Refers to all laws, regulations, principles, procedures, and their implementations that are broadly disseminated to ministries, institutions or public entities and the public.
Turnover tax	Paid every month at the rate of 2 per cent of the monthly turnover and implemented only on taxpayers in the Estimated Regime (to be abolished in 2016).
Value Added Tax (VAT)	Tax collected and paid by self-assessment regime taxpayers who make and supply taxable supplies (other than land or money) to their customers and the import of goods into the customs territory of the Kingdom of Cambodia. The VAT due is the difference between Output VAT (collected when supplying goods or services) and Input VAT (paid on import of goods or purchase of goods or services).
VAT Compliance Gap	The difference, in a given year, between the actual VAT paid and the estimated amount of VAT that should have been paid, i.e., total VAT theoretically due. Also known as the "VAT gap".
Withholding Tax	Tax withheld by resident taxpayers carrying on business who make payment in cash or in kind on income received by both resident and non-resident taxpayers from the performance of services, royalties, interest, income from the rental of movable and immovable, and dividends.
Wrongdoing	Tax administration wrongdoing includes inappropriate behaviour of its employees, especially the misuse of public office for personal gain (i.e., corruption).

Index

A

Accounts Payable (AP) Module, 83, 86
Accounts Receivable (AR) Module, 83, 85
Accrual-based Accounting, 80, 152
ADKAR Model (Awareness–Desire–Knowledge–Ability–Reinforcement), 93
Angkor Institution, 66
Annual Audit Plans, 131
Annual budget
  Cycle, 47–48, 50, 52
  Formulation, 47
  Review and approval of, 52–53
  Structure, 50
Annual Budget Law, 51–52
Annual Performance Report (APR), 33
Anti-Corruption Commission, 150
ASEAN, 1, 6–7, 9, 68, 137
Asian Financial Crisis, 3, 9, 137, 150
Asian Development Bank (ADB), 7, 18, 20, 41, 76, 126, 131
Audit Procedure Framework, 131
Australia, and performance budgeting, 160–63, 169
Australia National Audit Office, 163
Australian Department of Foreign Affairs and Trade (DFAT), 18
Automated System for Customs Data (ASYCUDA), 83, 86

B

Bilateral Aid, 7, 74, 130
Blended Finance, 72
Bond Market, 15, 74–75
Budget Act, 33, 157–58, 164
Budget Allocation (BA) Module, 83, 85
Budget Planning Module (BP) Module, 88
Budget Policy Statement, 153
Budget Review Act, 157–58
Budget Strategic Plan (BSP), 20, 27, 30, 42, 44–48, 53, 56, 127–29, 134
Budget System Reform Strategy (BSRS), 5, 28, 42, 44, 77, 79, 133
Budget System Reform Strategy for Subnational Administration, 28–29
Budget Transparency, 107, 113–15, 122
Bureau of the Budget (BoB), 138–39
Business Process Reengineering (BPR), 25
Business Process Streamlining, 92

C

Cambodia
  Budget information, 115
  Economic overview of, 8–11
  Foreign direct investment (FDI) in, 9, 15
  Formation of, 9
  GDP, 10, 13, 15, 23, 58, 60–61, 70, 97
  Independence, 8
  Open Budget Survey, 115–16
  PFM reform program (PFMRP) in, 13–17
  Public finance in, 11–13
  Regime change, 8
Cambodian Public Sector Accounting Standards (CPSAS), 79
Capital Expenditure, 45–46, 67–68, 70, 97, 130
Capital Revenue, 59–60, 67
Capitalism, 5
Cash-based Accounting, 77, 79
Cash Basis CPSAS (CB CPSAS), 79
Cash Basis IPSAS, 81
Cash Management (CA) Module, 85, 87
Central Budget Authority (CBA), 158, 170
Change Agent, 152, 170
Change Management, 39, 41, 44, 93, 149, 152
  Definition of, 170
Chart of Accounts (COA), 77–78, 127
Civil Aviation, 66
Civil Service, 6, 38–39, 68, 160
Civil War, 8
Collective Economy, 9
Commercial off-the-shelf (COTS) IT system, 151
Commonwealth Financial Accountability Review, 162
Communication and Engagement Strategy, 168
Communism, 5
Compliance Audit, 96
Consolidated Action Plan (CAP), 22
Control Systems, 57, 93–96
Core Taxes, 121–22
Corruption, 95, 114, 150, 152
Council for the Development of Cambodia (CDC), 46, 130
Council of Ministers, 45, 47
COVID-19 Pandemic, 10, 13, 23, 27, 43, 56–57
Cross-cutting Reform Programs, 36–40
Current Expenditure, 11–12, 67–68, 133
Current Revenue, 58–60
Customs and Excise Revenue, 61–63
Customs Reform and Modernization Program, 61
Cybersecurity, 166

D

Debt Management and Financial Analysis System (DMFAS), 83, 86
Decentralization and De-concentration (D&D), 6, 36–37, 39, 129, 132
Democratic Kampuchea Regime, 8
Department for International Development (DFID), 18
Department of Conservation, 155
Department of Corrections, 154, 156
Development Partners Committee (DPC), 16
Directorate General for Treasury, 152

Direct Performance Budgeting, 33
Document of Settlement, 96
Doi Moi, 140–41
Dollarized Economy, 10, 14–15
Domestic Revenue Mobilization, 57–59

E

Economic and Finance Institute (EFI), 131
Economic and Financial Policy Committee (EFPC), 15
Economic Transformation Program (ETP), 146
Education Management Information System (EMIS), 126–27, 135
Education Strategic Plan (ESP), 125
Effective Financial Accountability, 130
Electronic Fund Transfer (EFT), 86
Electronic Government Procurement (e-GP), 77
Electronic ID Card, 166
Emerging Markets Investor Alliance, 123
e-Police Systems, 167
e-Residency, 166–67
Estonia
  e-government, 165–67, 169
  Population, 165
E-Tax filing system, 166
European Development Cooperation Strategy for Cambodia, 19
European Joint Strategy, 19
European Union (EU), 18–20, 41, 68, 98

F

"Family-run Economy", 9

Financial Audit, 96
Financial Inspection System, 93, 95
Financial Management Improvement Plan (FMIP), 161–62
Financial Management Information System (FMIS), 14, 18–19, 21–23, 25–26, 52, 77, 127, 129, 131, 133, 135, 168
Financial Management Work Group, 92
Financial Reform Committee, 150
Financing Agreement, 20
Fiscal Responsibility Act, 153, 170
FMIS Budget Allocation Module, 88
France, and performance budgeting, 156–60, 169
Free Trade Agreement, 62
French Statistics Service, 159

G

Galing Pook Awards Program, 145
Gender Equality, 163–65, 169
General Department of Budget (GDB), 43, 54, 91
General Department of Customs and Excise (GDCE), 61–62
General Department of Financial Industry, 65
General Department of Inspection, 91
General Department of Internal Audit, 91
General Department of International Cooperation and Debt Management, 91
General Department of National Treasury (GDNT), 18, 78–79, 81, 83, 86–88, 91
General Department of Public Procurement, 91

General Department of State
    Property and Non-Tax Revenue
    (GDSPNR), 65, 75
General Department of Subnational
    Administration Finance
    (GDSNAF), 91, 132–33, 136
General Department of Taxation
    (GDT), 61, 63
General Departmental Action Plan
    (GDAP), 16
General Ledger (GL) Module, 86, 89
Global Financial Crisis, 10, 140
Global Initiative for Fiscal
    Transparency, 113
Globalization, 157
Government Finance Statistics (GFS),
    102–3
Government Financial Management
    and Revenue Administration
    Project (GFMRAP), 150–51
Government Transformation Program
    (GTP), 146

H
Human Capital, 31
Hun Sen, 13

I
Income Tax, 61, 63, 163
Independent Audit, 95–96
Independent Complaints Handling
    Mechanism, 77
Indonesia
    GDP, 149–50
    New financial system, 149–52
Industrial Development Policy (IDP),
    10
Inflation, 9–10, 24, 43, 141

Integrated Financial Management
    Information System (IFMIS),
    see SPAN
Integrated Offender Management, 154
Internal Audit, 23, 27, 91, 93–96
Internal Audit Department (IAD),
    127, 130–31, 135
Internal Audit Manual (IAM), 131
Internal Revenue Allotment (IRA),
    145, 169
International Budget Partnership
    (IBP), 112, 114, 123
International Financial Reporting
    Standards (IFRSs), 77
International Monetary Fund (IMF),
    18, 21, 32, 72–73, 97, 102,
    113–14, 116
International Organization of Supreme
    Audit Institutions, 113
International Public Sector
    Accounting Standards (IPSAS),
    14, 20, 77–79
i-Voting, 167

J
Japan International Cooperation
    Agency (JICA), 21

K
Khmer Republic Regime, 8
Khmer Rouge Regime, 8, 14

L
Land Transport Safety Authority, 154
Law of Audit of the RGC, 95
Law on Administrative Management
    of the Capital, Provinces,
    Municipalities, Districts, and
    Khans, 36, 132

Law on Commune and Sangkat Administration and Management, 36, 132
Law on Public Financial Management and Budget Strategic Frameworks, 134
Law on Public Financial Systems, 30, 52, 67
Law on the Management and Use of State Assets, 142
Lehman Brothers, 159
Lima Declaration of Guidelines on Auditing Precepts, 113
Local Government Code (LGC), 143–45, 168
Local Government Units (LGUs), 144–46
LOLF (*Loi organique relative aux lois de finance*), 157–60

M
Malaysia, and outcome-based budgeting, 33, 146–49
Malaysia Plan, 147, 170
Maori Education Strategy, 155
Medium-Term Budget Framework (MTBF), 27, 43–46, 48, 54, 56, 134
Medium-Term Expenditure Framework (MTEF), 138–40
Medium-Term Fiscal Framework (MTFF), 27, 42–43, 48, 54, 56
Medium-Term Investment Plan (MTIP), 142
Medium-Term Macroeconomic and Public Finance Framework (MMPFF), 42, 48, 54
Medium-Term Revenue Mobilization Strategy, 58

Middle-Income Trap, 146
Mining, 66
Ministerial Action Plan (MAP), 16, 125–26
Ministry of Civil Service, 36
Ministry of Economy and Finance (MEF), 16, 20–21, 23, 25, 27, 40–41, 45, 47–48, 60, 67–68, 75, 88, 90–92, 111, 116, 125–32, 135
   Non-tax revenue, 65–66
   Procurement regulator, 30, 76–77
   Technical support, 53
Ministry of Education, New Zealand, 155
Ministry of Education, Youth, and Sport (MOEYS), 7, 54–55
   Budget allocation for, 124–25
   Public Financial Management Reform Program (PFMRP), 124–28, 135
Ministry of Finance, 33
Ministry of Finance (MoF), Indonesia, 150–51
Ministry of Finance (MoF), Malaysia, 147–48
Ministry of Finance (MoF), Vietnam, 141–42
Ministry of Health (MOH), 124
Ministry of Interior (MOI), 37, 124, 135
Ministry of National Defence (MOD), 124
Ministry of Planning, 46, 130
Ministry of Planning and Investment (MPI), Vietnam, 141–42
Ministry of Rural Development (MRD), 7, 124
Ministry of Women's Affairs, 88

Modified Budgeting System (MBS), 147
Multi-donor Trust Fund, 18, 21
Multilateral Aid, 7, 130

N

National Accounting Council (NAC), 79
National Assembly, 47, 52, 88, 95–96, 115, 170
National Audit Authority (NAA), 94–95, 131
National Bank of Cambodia (NBC), 11, 15–16, 86
National Budget Office (NBO), 148
National Committee for Democratic Development (NCDD), 37, 132
National OBB Steering Committee (NOSC), 148
National Policy on Indigenous Peoples' Development, 129
National Program for Administrative Reform (NPAR), 36, 38
National Program for Public Administration Reform, 39
National Program for Subnational Democratic Development, 36
National Social Protection, 24
National Strategy Development Plan (NSDP), 43, 46, 48, 51, 128–29, 134
National Sustainable Development Plan (NSDP), 22
National Transformation Program (NTP), 146
National Treasury, 65–66, 75, 126
New Budget System, 53–54
New Political Economy of PFM, 4

New Public Financial Management (NPFM), 4–5
New Public Management, 138, 140, 147
New Zealand
  Currency crisis, 3
  Outcome-focus management, 152–56, 169
New Zealand Biodiversity Strategy, 155
Non-Tax Revenue, 65–66
Non-Tax Revenue Management Information System (NRMIS), 65–66, 83, 86

O

OECD, 1, 6–7, 33, 76, 113, 137
OECD Survey of Gender Budgeting, 164
Official Development Assistance (ODA), 15, 74
Open Budget Survey (OBS), 7, 99, 122
Organic Financial Law, see LOLF
Outcome-based Budgeting (OBB), 33, 146–49, 168
Output Agreement, 154

P

Paris Declaration, 18
Paris Peace Accord, 11, 14
People's Republic of Kampuchea (PRK), see Cambodia
Performance Audit, 96
Performance-based Budgeting (PBB), 5, 32–33, 138, 146
Performance Budgeting Model, 32–34
Performance-Informed Budgeting (PIB), 5, 22, 32, 34–36, 96

PFM Reform Steering Committee (PFMR-SC), 14, 16, 20, 40, 53
PFM Technical Working Group (PFM-TWG), 16
Philippines
   Annual growth, 143
   Decentralization, 143–46
   Government system, 144
   Platform approach, 14
Political Dynasty, 146
Poverty, 10, 15, 103, 128, 140, 143–46
Prakas, 66, 75
Principles for Public Participation in Fiscal Policy, 113
Problem-Driven Analysis, 6
Procurement Module, 90
Procurement Review Committee (PRC), 76
Program-based Budgeting (PBB), 20–21
Program Budgeting Review, 31
Program Operating Budgets (BOPs), 158
Program Performance Budgeting System (PPBS), 147
Public Accounting System, 77–81
Public Administration Entities (PAEs), 90
Public Administrative Reform, 16, 38–39, 129
Public Debt Management, 74–75, 97
Public Expenditure and Financial Accountability (PEFA), 7, 76, 97
   Assessment, 105–12
   Framework, 99–103, 121–22
   Performance indicators, 103–5
   Subnational level, at, 105, 133
Public Expenditure Management (PEM), 67–70

Public Finance Act, 3
Public Financial Management Modernization Project, 18
Public Financial Management (PFM)
   Assessment tools, 99
   Components of, 57
   Definition, 2–3
   Seven pillars of, 100–102
   Subnational Administrations, and, 132–35
   Theories of, 4–6
Public Financial Management Reform Program (PFMRP)
   Achievements, 23–25
   Budget system, 30–36
   Challenges, 25–26
   Donors, 18–19
   Implementation, 21–22
   Ministry of Education, Youth and Sport (MOEYS), impact on, 124–28, 135
   Ministry of Rural Development (MRD), impact on, 128–31, 135
Public Governance, Performance and Accountability Act (PGPA Act), 160–62
Public Infrastructure, expenditure on, 70–72
Public Investment Law, 168
Public Investment Management (PIM), 45, 47, 70–73, 97, 142–43, 168
Public Investment Management Assessment (PIMA), 7, 99, 116–20, 122
Public Investment Management System Reform Strategy, 28–29, 72

Public Investment Program (PIP), 46, 130
Public Investment System Reform Strategy, 168
Public-Private Partnerships (PPPs), 72–73, 117, 120
Public Procurement Management, 75–77
Public Procurement System Reform Strategy, 28, 30
Public Sector Management Reform Plan (PSMRP), 137
Purchase Agreement, 170
Purchase Order (PO) Module, 86, 88

R

Rectangular Strategy (RS), 13, 26, 43, 48, 51, 129
Resource Leaders Training (RLT), 149
Results-Based Management System, 35
Revenue
  Capital, 59–60, 67
  Current, 58–60
  Customs and excise, 61–63
  Non-tax, 65–66
  Tax, 60–61, 63–64, 97
  Types of, 59–60
Revenue Mobilization Strategy, 28–29, 59, 63, 65–66, 96–97
Road Investment, 70
Road Safety Strategy, 154
Rocard, Michel, 157
Royal Decree, 15, 25
Russia-Ukraine War, 11

S

Sangkum Reastr Niyum Regime, 8
Senate, 47, 52, 95–96, 144

Seven Budget Classifications, 90–91
SMART goals, 154
Socialism, 5
Socio-Economic Development Plan (SEDP), 141
Soviet-style Planned Economy, 9
SPAN (*Sistem Perbendaharaan dan Anggaran Negara*), 151, 168, 170
Special Drawing Rights (SDR), 97
Standard Operational Procurements for PPP, 72
State Asset Register Management Information System (SARMIS), 66, 75
State Audit Office, 160
State Budget Law (SBL), 142
State Economy, 9
State-Owned Enterprises (SOEs), 9
State Property Management, 27, 75
State Sector Act 1988, 153
Strategic Audit Plans, 131
Strategic Performance-based Budgeting (SPBB), 34
Strategic Plan for Thai Public Sector Development, 140
Strategic Plan on Streamlining Business Process, 92
Strengthening Public Financial Management Program (SPFMP), 20
Subnational Administrations (SNAs), 7, 37–39
  Public Financial Management (PFM), and, 132–35
Supreme Audit Institution (SAI), 95–96, 112
Sustainable Development Goals, 128–29

Swedish Gender Equality Agency, 164
Swedish International Development Cooperation Agency (SIDA), 18–19

T
Tax Administration Diagnostic Assessment Tool (TADAT), 7, 99
  Framework, 120–22
Tax Evasion, 61–62, 64–65
Tax Reform, 63–65
Tax Revenue, 60–61, 63–64, 97
Tax System, 86
Thailand
  GDP, 137
  Strategic Performance-based Budgeting, 137–40, 167
Thaksin Shinawatra, 139–40
Tourism, 57, 66, 144
Transportation Improvements, comparison of, 69
Treasury Single Account, 25

U
United Nations, 7, 14
United Nations Children's Fund (UNICEF), 18, 20–21, 126
United Nations Transitional Authority in Cambodia (UNTAC), 14
US Planning, Programming and Budgeting System, 156

V
VAT, 63
Vietnam
  GDP, 140
  Public Investment Management, 140–43
Vision and Strategy for 3+1 Reform Program, 40

W
Wartime Economy, 8
White Paper, 150, 170
World Bank, 7, 9, 11, 18, 35, 53, 98, 126, 131, 138, 142, 150–51
World Customs Organization, 123
WTO, 9

X
"X-Road" project, 166

www.ingramcontent.com/pod-product-compliance
Lightning Source LLC
Chambersburg PA
CBHW071355290426
44108CB00014B/1560